OPIVM FOR THE MASSES

HARVESTING NATURE'S BEST
PAIN MEDICATION BY JIM HOGSHIRE

FERAL HOUSE

OPIUM FOR THE MASSES: Harvesting Nature's Best Pain Medication
© 2009 by Jim Hogshire. The earlier edition of this book was published in 1994
by the currently defunct Loompanics Unlimited.

ISBN: 978-1-932595-46-8

❦

A Feral House Original Paperback.
Feral House
1240 W. Sims Way Suite 124
Port Townsend, WA 98368
www.FeralHouse.com

❦

TABLE OF CONTENTS

℞ *Throchiscorum Stiliticorum* ℥ xij ,
    Viperinorum ,
  Magmatis Hedycroi ,   *Therebinthinæ Chiæ* , ana ℥ j ß ,
  Piperis longi ,   *Radicum Gentianæ* ,
  Opÿ Thebaici , ana ℥ vj ,
  Rosarum rubrarum ,   *Acori Veri* ,
  Iridis ,   *Meu Athamantici* ,
     Valerianæ majoris ,
  Succi Glycyrrhizæ ,   *Nardi Celticæ* ,
  Seminis Buniadis ,   *Amomi racemosi* ,
  Scordij ,   *Chamæpytheos* ,
  Opobalsami ,   *Comæ Hyperici* ,
  Cinnamomi ,   *Seminis Ameos* ,
  Agarici , ana ℥ iij ,   *Thlaspeos* ,
  Costi ,   *Anisi* ,
  Nardi Indicæ ,   *Faniculi* ,
  Dictamini Cretici ,   *Siseleos Massiliensis* ,
  Rhapontici ,   *Cardamomi minoris* ,
  Radicis Pentaphylli ,   *Malabathri*
    Zinziberis ,   *Comæ Polij montani* ,
  Prassÿ albi ,   *Chamædryos* ,
  Stœchadis Arabicæ ,   *Carpobalsami* ,
  Schænanthi ,   *Succi Hypocistidos* ,
  Seminis Petroselini Macedonici ,   *Acaciæ Veræ* ,
  Calamintha montanæ ,   *Gummi Arabici* ,
  Cassiæ ligneæ ,   *Styracis Calamitæ* ,
  Croci ,   *Terræ Lemniæ* ,
  Piperis albi ,   *Chalcitidis* ,
    Nigri ,   *Sagapeni* ana ℥ j ,
  Mirræ Trogloditidis ,   *Radicum Aristolochiæ tenuis* ,
  Thuris masculi ,   *Comæ Centaurij minoris* ,
     Seminis Dauci Cretici ,
     Opopanacis ,
     Galbani ,
     Bituminis Iudaïci ,
     Castores ana ℥ ß ,
     Mellis optimi despumati ℔ xxviij ,
     Vini generosi quantùm satis.

From the *Pharmacopée Royale* of 1676.

CHAPTER 1
ROMANTIC POETS
AND DOPE FIENDS

Everything one does in life, even love, occurs in an express train racing toward death. To smoke opium is to get out of the train while it is still moving. It is to concern oneself with something other than life or death.

— Jean Cocteau, *Opium* —

JUST THE SOUND OF ITS NAME, *OPIUM*, EVOKES AN EXOTIC, seductive feeling. Gorgeous dreams and a quiet undertone of fear. Milk of Paradise, Plant of Joy, Destroyer of Grief: these are opium's poetic nicknames.

Homer wrote of the drug in *The Iliad* and *The Odyssey* three thousand years ago. Since then, writers have praised opium for its seemingly divine properties. Victorian writers, particularly, are famous for their love of opium. Poets sought to describe the feeling opium gave them with otherworldly imagery. One writer said opium felt like "walking through silk." Opium devotees have an unashamed and tender passion for their drug.

"Who was the man who invented laudanum?" wrote a nineteenth-century British author for the opiated drink. "I thank him from the bottom of my heart..."

"I have had six delicious hours of oblivion; I have woken up with my mind composed ... and all through the modest little bottle of drops which I see on my bedroom chimneypiece at this moment. Drops, you are darling! If I love nothing else, I love you!"

ROMEO AND JULIET PALE BESIDE SUCH ROMANCE

FALLING IN LOVE WITH OPIUM IS EASY. OPIUM ALWAYS DELIVERS ON ITS promise. Smoked, eaten or drunk, opium never fails to banish fatigue and pain, to stimulate the mind and liberate the user from nervousness or worry. Another British gentleman of the nineteenth-century said opium felt something like a gentle and constant orgasm! It gave him the same feeling he experienced at the end of a successful day and made the most mechanical tasks seem interesting. Such a drug is sure to have its fans.

America's appetite for opium grew steadily throughout the nineteenth and twentieth centuries. In 1914 a San Francisco newspaperman described his first encounter with the drug in an opium den in Chinatown. Although he had previously shunned the stuff as a drug of the yellow hordes, he at last relented and breathed a huge lungful of opium smoke.

"In sixty seconds I was another man," he wrote. "My barren brain... leaped to its task. The ideas, the phrases, the right words, which, until then, had eluded my fagged mentality, came trooping forth faster than I could have written them had I been at my desk. My worries and responsibilities fell from me..."

"A half hour later I wrote a column of dramatic criticism that was quoted on the billboards and I reeled it off as fast as my fingers could hit the typewriter keys. I was never at a loss for a word. The story in its entirety seemed to lie ready in my brain. My task finished, I went to bed without my customary drink, and dropped asleep as peacefully as a child... I slept soundly and awoke refreshed and clear-minded with a zest for the day's labor."

Opium's ability to banish sadness, relieve pain, and energize the soul borders on the miraculous. Opium can release the most wretched from life's worst agonies. A nineteenth-century physician, Horace Day, mentions opium when describing the ghastly post-Civil War American countryside. Amid all that suffering, this plant sap could offer refuge to displaced, half-dead people:

Maimed and shattered survivors from a hundred battlefields, diseased and disabled soldiers released from hostile prisons, anguished and hopeless wives and mothers, made so by the slaughter of those who were dearest to them, have found, many of them, temporary relief from their sufferings in opium.

❖

A love affair with opium cannot be taken lightly. The same poppy that can take its lovers to the gates of paradise has the power to send its slaves to a hell on earth, should they ever try to leave her.

Today the word "yen" means a kind of longing or desire. But its origin—from the Chinese *yenyen*—describes something more desperate: the torture of opium withdrawal. To yen for opium is to feel an intense lack of everything—of sanity, soul, and body—but mostly of opium.

Yen conjures up the image of a contorted, sweat-soaked figure writhing on rumpled bedsheets. Addicts kicking opium have described feeling as if their nerves were afire—"a thousand needles popping through the skin." The body becomes a bloodless slab of pain.

Sleep is plagued with baroque nightmares and wakefulness feels worse. Muscles contract, so arms and legs jerk and kick without warning. This last feature of the yen has given us the expression "kicking." Worse, there is a definite and palpable emotional aspect of the suffering. Just as its presence is so often equated with being in love, its absence creates a void in the heart of the withdrawing user that is similar to a broken heart.

"It's like having the worst case of the flu," says a friend of mine, "and getting brutally dumped by your girlfriend at the same time."

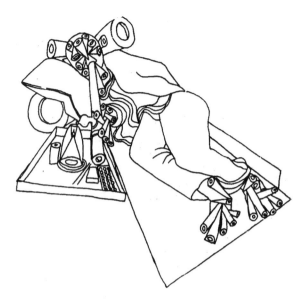

THE OPIUM PIPE SMOKER BY JEAN COCTEAU.

OPIUM ADDICTION: AN HONEST DISCLAIMER

❖

It is not I who become addicted, it is my body.

— Jean Cocteau, *Opium* —

❖

"If an addict who has been completely cured starts smoking again he no longer experiences the discomfort of his first addiction. There exists, therefore, outside alkaloids and habit, a sense for opium, an intangible habit which lives on, despite the recasting of the organism… The dead drug leaves a ghost behind. At certain hours it haunts the house."

— Jean Cocteau, *Opium* —

Physical dependence on opium is a virtual certainty with prolonged and sustained use. There may be a psychological dependence to opium but that bears no relationship to the drug per se and has more to do with a user's personality than anything else. The chances of psychological addiction to opium are no greater than with alcohol or marijuana.

Psychological problems are beyond the scope of this book. You know if you've got a problem—with shopping, compulsive lying, or substance abuse. This book is about opium and its children, so its physical addiction must be addressed—but "addiction" has become a term so freighted with social and political connotations that it is almost irresponsible to use the term in a book like this. Physical dependence will be the result of opium use sooner or later, but it doesn't necessarily develop quickly, nor must it last forever.

Opium withdrawal hurts, but the pain (including the intense, broken-hearted feeling of loss) will end within a week to ten days. That's how long the body needs to get shocked back into producing the chemicals replaced with constant opium use. Those are indeed hard days for the kicking addict but it is no worse than a nasty and prolonged flu. And like the flu, once the pain goes, it's over. The user feels no more physical craving for the drug.

The psychological aspect of addiction might impose itself, and it could be at least several months before an ex-user feels himself again.

This is even true of heroin, as William Burroughs says in his candid novel-autobiography *Junky*. Burroughs says that once a junkie has kicked, it is easy to stay away from junk. This said, it should be noted that Burroughs was a lifelong heroin addict. So it is with opium, from which heroin is derived.

"Relapse" is another phenomenon loaded with social connotations. For many people life is simply better with opium than without it—that they should seek it is hardly surprising. Addiction to caffeine, for instance, has all the same features of opium addiction. Dependence develops, withdrawal hurts and then you get used to life without coffee.

Some people decide to go back to drinking coffee, some just abstain for a while and go back—but the lack of coffee rarely preys on their minds so much they cannot stay away.

It is difficult to become physically dependent on opium in the first place. Before the body becomes truly dependent on opium (so that abstinence produces withdrawal symptoms) a user must take opium on a daily basis for at least a month or two. It takes this long for the body to "learn" to stop producing its own opiate chemicals and become dependent on an outside source. The amount of time needed to induce dependence or withdrawal differs among the various derivatives of opium or its alkaloids. In general, the longer acting the opiate drug the longer it takes for withdrawal symptoms to develop after the last use and the longer they tend to last (although they are usually milder). As with almost anything related to the subject, there are few simple or rigid "rules." Opium is too complex, too subtle.

Society's fascination with addiction has propelled scientists (and the government functionaries who fund their research) to discover new ways to both prevent addiction from occurring and to ease an addict off of opiates with practically no pain at all. In recent years a new therapy known as "ultra-rapid detox" has become popular because it can collapse all of the pain and lethargy of the first week or ten days abstinence into just four hours. Since it is done under general anesthesia, the addict shouldn't feel a thing, or suffer in the least. In theory, at least.

These latest methods of kicking an opiate addiction are not yet perfect. Nor are they inexpensive.

WHO'S A HOPHEAD?

IN COUNTRIES WHERE OPIUM IS FREELY AVAILABLE, IT IS PLAIN TO SEE THAT A portion of the population enjoys taking opium. It has been this way for thousands of years and opium has yet to impede civilization or cause it any harm.

Opium use in America rose steadily from Benjamin Franklin poppy consumption days until 1915 when it suddenly became illegal. Despite the fact that at least one out of ten Americans was addicted—a number cutting across all class and social lines—the U.S. was a prosperous nation. Universities were founded, science advanced, commerce blossomed, public works were carried out. By any measure of progress or success the United States became in all ways more prosperous when drugs were legal.

It could be argued that the age of prohibitions that started in the twentieth century has brought us more misery.

Dosage is a highly individual decision. This dose can vary within a certain range but generally stays the same and isn't necessarily high. Use tends to increase at first, then plateau. Although tolerance can develop quickly or slowly, it is not an inexorable upward spiral toward impossible amounts of the drug and exorbitant consumption.

Most people, when allowed free access to any particular drug, do not go bananas over it. The use of alcohol in our society is proof of that. Most people don't drink alcohol all the time. Same goes for coffee.

Pharmacologically, opium use is also self-regulating. When eaten, it is subject to a "first pass" through the liver where a considerable amount is inactivated. Larger amounts to compensate for this effect begin to pose a physical problem for the user—one can only swallow so much opium before getting sick, or at least getting full! Smoked, even less of the active parts gets through to the bloodstream and, once again, increasing the dose poses practical problems.

Still, the pleasure provided by opium makes continuous use fairly easy to accomplish. Most addicts know that, once free of the drug's physical hold, it is enough to skip a day or two between uses to avoid re-addiction.

ALL THOSE FAMOUS ADDICTS

POETIC TESTIMONIALS TO OPIUM HAVE TYPICALLY BEEN USED TO DEFEND opium use. When such brilliant minds as Ben Franklin and Thomas de Quincey use opium, the argument goes, isn't it obvious that it is harmless? Drug-use promoters of the 1960s seemed to constantly thump the cover of a copy of de Quincey's *Confessions of an English Opium Eater* while making the case for marijuana. But marijuana is not like opium and neither is it like heroin, although heroin comes closer. Heroin is an opiate (derived from opium) elaborated from morphine but it is pharmacologically quite distinct from opium. Later incarnations of the morphine molecule are even less like opium.

Opium addiction—as we now define it—played no part in the lives of opium users before the twentieth century. Even as society began to criminalize opium and heap scorn on its user, the word "addict" was not used. At the time, doctors spoke of "habitués"—and without alarm. And why should they? Opium does not cause any harm to the body. Opium users still got up in the morning and went to work, had families, and paid their bills. What was there to be upset about?

Dependence on opium was observed but was not associated with the same kinds of value judgments as it is today. An addict was not a "dope fiend" or any other kind of antisocial monster. Opium addiction was not viewed as a particularly good thing and many addicts denied or hid their dependence. Many tried hard to kick the habit.

They tried to kick because, in their world as in ours, dependence was a negative trait. Perhaps it indicated a lack of moral fortitude or implied some other kind of weakness. But opium addiction, like alcohol addiction, was not criminal. Opium addiction wasn't considered important in any medical sense. Doctors often remarked of their patients who tried to shake the habit that they could see no reason for all the trouble. Since opium did not interfere with their lives or health—so what?

Those who liked opium took it. Those who didn't like it didn't take it.

So to speak of Edgar Allan Poe—"opium addict" is next to useless, since this feature of his life probably meant as much or as little to him as any other facet.

In my opinion, the biggest problem of opium addiction is one of supply. Any others (social ostracism, criminal sanctions, etc.) are man-made quandaries.

Opiate dependence—especially if used to control chronic pain—does not interfere with normal life. Those with an adequate supply do not suffer as long as they have the drug. Sick people suffer if they do not have it. History is full of famous opium addicts whose habits did not interfere with their lives.

For many, the good to be gained from opium far outweighs its potential dangers. And, like other opium fans, I defy anyone to compare the destruction wrought by the natural consequences of drinking alcohol with whatever minimal difficulties may be caused by opium use. It is no longer disputed that opium or opiates do any harm to the body. Nineteenth-century physicians spoke openly about deliberately hooking their alcoholic patients on morphine as an effective way to end the damage chronic alcohol drinking caused. Opium is even more innocuous than morphine and I challenge those who still believe opium is a tool of the devil to show me a shred of serious evidence that opium is any more harmful than carrots.

A Minoan goddess wearing poppy capsules as hairpins; the vertical slits in the capsules are stained brown like opium. This little statue (78 cm) was found in a secluded setting suggestive of opium smoking (c. 1300 - 1250 B. C.). (From *The Healing Hand* by Guido Maino, Harvard University Press, 1975.)

CHAPTER 1 ❖ ROMANTIC POETS & DOPE FIENDS

THE ORIGINS AND HISTORY OF OPIUM

FOSSILIZED POPPY SEEDS AND OTHER ARCHEOLOGICAL EVIDENCE FOUND IN digs near lakes in Switzerland reveals that the opium poppy was used by Neanderthal man as long as 30,000 years ago. Prehistoric use of poppies could have gone beyond the use of opium, as the poppy yields abundant quantities of nutritious seed, which can be eaten raw or cooked. The dried plant also provides a clean-burning fuel, and poppy straw is still used today for animal fodder. Its drug qualities could have also fulfilled a religious role of some kind—a theory that has gained credence in recent years.

Sumerian ideograms from about 4,000 B.C. refer to the poppy as the "plant of joy" (HUL - GIL). In some parts of the world, variations on the word "Gil" are still used to say "opium." Opium poppies were cultivated for millennia by the civilizations of Mesopotamia, Persia and in ancient Egypt. Opium use in ancient Egypt is a disputed topic for some reason, but the evidence is pretty substantial. Opium is mentioned in the Ebers papyrus (dating from around 1500 B.C.) and traces of opium seem to have been found in the tomb of the ancient Egyptian chief royal architect Kha, who died about 1405 B.C. Hieroglyphics from only a hundred years later are not disputed, however, as they turn up clear references to opium—especially as a drug to make babies stop crying.

In Greece, especially, the poppy occupied an important place in medicine and mythology. Hippocrates describes the opium poppy in his medical writings of around 400 B.C. Centuries later (c. 55–70 A.D.) another Greek physician, Dioscorides, who lived and worked in Rome, conducted methodical comparison studies with the juice of the poppyhead (opium) and extracts made from the whole plant. These tests showed it was opium, the juice of the poppyhead, that had the greatest effects in comparison with concoctions of the entire plant. Opium might have been called the "active ingredient" in the poppy plant.

Dioscorides must have thought there was something useful in the rest of the plant, however, because his best-known contribution to the cornucopia of opium medicines was an extract he called *diacodion*, using the Greek word for "poppyhead." The same word was used to name codeine, when that alkaloid was first isolated in 1832. Diacodion remained in use as a standard medicine, later referred to as "syrup of poppies," for centuries afterward.

One of the last of the Greek physicians, Galen (who shaped European medicine for several hundred years), gushed over opium's properties in his medical treatises, reporting how it was brought to mankind by the bird-headed Egyptian god Thoth. But Galen also flatly denied the plant was "magical." The good doctor prescribed it for cough, diarrhea, and to relieve pain. He recommended opium to calm an agitated patient, and to help insomniacs get some sleep. Galen also considered opium an antidote for poisons in general—snake venom in particular. Other items on his list of conditions treatable with some preparation of opium were deafness, failing eyesight and vertigo.

In *The Odyssey*, Homer described how Helen of Troy livened up some would-be partiers who were grieving over dead or missing loved ones when she added opium to the wine they were drinking. This combo, the poet said, would "lull all pain and anger, and bring forgetfulness of every sorrow."

The mythological Greek goddess of agriculture, Demeter, searching for her daughter Persephone came to a place once known as "city of poppies." It was there that she discovered that by tasting the gum oozing from the poppy capsule, she was immediately relieved of her sadness. Because of this, ancient Greek drawings of Demeter often portray her holding a small bouquet of poppies.

"Whoever drinks a draught thereof," he wrote, "on that day no tear would fall down his cheeks, not even if his mother and his father died, not even if men slew his brother or dear son with the sword, before his own eyes."—*The Odyssey*, Book IV

Other Greek gods were shown with poppies, including Nyx (goddess of night), Hypnos (god of sleep), Morpheus (god of dreams), and Thanatos (god of death). Morpheus, of course, became the namesake to opium's principle alkaloid: morphine.

❖

Opium's power to produce fantastic dreams of astonishing clarity was certainly well known long ago, as this passage from the Greek writer Lucin's true history shows us. Traveling to the Isle of Dreams, Lucin and friends visit the island's port city, called "Sleep" or "Slumber."

One Greek word for opium is *mekon* or *mekone*, the latter being the name of the prehistoric city later known as Kyllene. The word *mekone* means something like "Poppy Town," is associated with Hermes, and is the place where Prometheus first brought fire to humans. Our own word, opium, comes from another Greek word—*opos*, meaning "liquid."

This Greek word now appears in many variations around the world. In Arabic the word for opium is *afioon* (Nryfa), in Urdu, *afim*, and *a-fou-yong* in some dialects of Chinese. Even the Chinese word *yen* (which describes more than one aspect of opium) appears to derive from Greek. And the Japanese word for "narcotic," *mayaku*, may be related to the Greek *mekone*. In any case, opium was not cultivated in Japan until the fifteenth century, so the plant may very well have a "foreign" name there. *Mekone* is the root for the word *mak* which refers to opium and to opium poppies in a number of eastern European languages including Russian, Czech, and even Romanian.

Images of poppy plants in ceremonial use can be found on coins and drawings in the ruins of past civilizations in Greece and other areas of the Mediterranean. Although it is said that opium smoking was not practiced by Europeans until the late fifteenth century (then perfected by the Chinese after that), ancient pipes found in Cyprus apparently used for opium date from the late Bronze age (c. 1200 B.C.). Vases from this same time period depict methods of incising the capsule to gather opium.

Two of many small juglets (top right, bottom left) that came to Egypt from Cyprus around 1600 - 1500 B.C., compared with poppy capsules (same scale). The similarity in size, shape and surface pattern suggests that these juglets were full of opium. Insert below shows scale.
(From *The Healing Hand* by Guido Majno, Harvard University Press, 1975).

CHAPTER 1 ❖ ROMANTIC POETS & DOPE FIENDS

As mentioned earlier, ancient Egyptian medicine made use of opium, and medical papyri describe hundreds of prescriptions containing opium. The substance appears in about a third of the formulas uncovered to date. Later on, the Egyptian city of Thebes became well-known for the opium it produced and sent out around the world. Hence, standard Egyptian opium was called *Thebic* opium. Today one of opium's most important alkaloids, thebaine, reminds us of this city. A Persian word for "cure-all"—*teriak*—also found its way into English as a name for an opium-based panacea-type medicine.

The Romans used opium extensively, and the drug was sold everywhere in the streets of the eternal city. The Roman poet Virgil mentions opium in his *Aeneid*, and one of Rome's most famous emperors, Marcus Aurelius, seems to have used opium frequently and regularly enough that he suffered from withdrawal symptoms if he went without, according to contemporary reports describing his well-being.

The famous Persian physician Abu 'Ali al Husein Ibn Sina (known in the West as Avicenna) was another proponent of opium, prescribing it to quiet crying babies, treat diarrhea, cough, anemia and other afflictions. Avicenna's medical work, *Canon of Medicine*, superseded Galen at the beginning of the Renaissance to become the basis for Western medicine right through the 1800s.

Avicenna also did extensive clinical testing of opium and was especially good at working out appropriate dosages and dosing schedules that allowed him to more effectively treat all the typical diseases, and then some. For instance, Avicenna took advantage of opium's tendency to lower blood sugar levels and used it to treat diabetes. In later centuries, morphine would be used in the same way, not displaced until the advent of insulin injections.

Persians, Turks, and Arabs all called the poppy flower *Qashqash* (or similar variations—the name imitates the sound of poppy seeds rattling around in the dried capsule) and poppies and opium were an important part of their systems of medicine, later adopted by the West.

As the spread of the word opium indicates, use of the poppy's juice dispersed outward from Greece and Asia Minor (Turkey), being mostly carried far and wide by the physicians and explorers of the Islamic world. The poppy was of great interest to the early Muslims because the Koran forbids alcohol, the only realistic alternative to opium at the time, especially for anaesthesia and pain relief. These Muslim physicians even developed an anaesthetic sponge that was soaked in a mixture of opium and hashish, water and inert carrier substances (usually wheat). The sponge was then allowed to dry, and could be quickly brought into use by wetting it again. Held over the mouth and nose of the patient, the sponge could render a patient sufficiently unconscious that surgeons could perform abdominal surgery. Of course, much of this knowledge was lost on medieval Europeans, who were busy waiting out the end of their Dark Ages.

Opium is mentioned in that enormous collection of stories dating back around a thousand years and known in the West as *The Arabian Nights* or *The Thousand and One Nights*. These stories mention another poppy confection people consumed to lighten their mood: Post. The word post is still used in Bangladesh, Burma and some other places, where it seems to refer to poppy seed—specifically poppy seed mixed with other spices, sugar, milk, and possibly hashish or marijuana.

By no later than the eighth century A.D. poppies and the use of opium had spread throughout Arabia, India, and China. Its northward journey took a bit longer, but by the eleventh century, opium was in use all over the Eurasian continent.

Although opium was known to medieval Europeans, the drug jumped in popularity at the end of the twelfth century, when Christian crusaders, returning from their attacks in the Middle East, brought back Avicenna's new medicines—along with silk, soap and remission from all their sins. Variations of a narcotic potion containing a large amount of opium was in widespread use in the later Middle Ages. In medieval

England we have a recipe for a knockout drink used to render a patient unconscious "while men carve him." The same or similar potions—sometimes called *dwale*—were simply used to bring on sleep in case of insomnia. Just such an opium-based medicine is mentioned by Geoffrey Chaucer in "The Reeve's Tale":

> *To bedde goth Alyn and also John*
> *Ther nas na moore—hem nedede no dwale.*

Chaucer refers directly to opium in another of *The Canterbury Tales*—this time in "The Knight's Tale"—where it is used to spike a jailer's drink, knocking him out and allowing a prisoner to escape. The escapee's daring pal seem to have left nothing to chance and used the best opium he could get his hands on. Chaucer tells us that the Thebian opium used was "fyn."

> *That soone after the mydnyght Palamon*
> *By helpyng of a freend brak his prison*
> *And fleeth the citee faste as he may go.*
> *For he hadde yeue his gailler drynke so*
> *Of a claree maad of certeyn wyn*
> *With nercotikes and opye of Thebes fyn*
> *That al that nyght, thogh that men wolde hym shake,*
> *The gailler sleep; he myghte noght awake.*
> *And thus he fleeth as faste as euere he may.*

Centuries later, Shakespeare refers to opium in *Othello*:

> *Not poppy, nor mandragore,*
> *Nor all the drowsy syrups of the world,*
> *Shall ever medicine thee to that sweet sleep*
> *Which thou ow'dst yesterday*

Opium's rediscovery helped make the careers of Renaissance doctors like Paracelsus (1490–1540) who referred to the stash of opium kept in his saddle as his "stone of immortality," using it for all those cases "when death is to be cheated." Paracelsus was also the inventor of laudanum (from Latin meaning "praised"), an opium preparation still in use today. Like dwale, laudanum had many permutations, but the original (probably in pill form) contained henbane, crushed pearls, frog sperm, and cinnamon, along with a healthy portion of opium.

Laudanum's next high-profile promoter was the English physician Thomas Sydenham (1624–1689) who simplified the recipe, making his laudanum by dissolving opium into alcohol—a method that remains the official preparation of laudanum into the early twentieth century.

Sydenham had unmitigated praise for opium. "Of all the remedies which the Almighty God has bestowed upon mankind, to lighten our miseries," he wrote, "there is none to equal opium in its power to moderate the violence of so many maladies, and even to cure some of them. Without opium, Medicine would be a one-armed man."

Another preparation of opium was invented by one of Sydenham's students, Thomas Dover, who had already contributed a footnote to Western cultural history in 1709, when he rescued a man named Alexander Selkirk, who had been stranded on a deserted island. News of this event inspired Daniel Defoe's character Robinson Crusoe.

After retiring on his swashbuckling booty, the 40-year-old Dover took up medicine, using opium in much larger doses than usually called for. But opium wasn't his favorite medicine. Dover was sometimes known as Dr. Quicksilver for his frequent and heavy prescribing of mercury. To make it easier to take his larger doses of opium, Dover invented an opium medicine that became famous as "Dover's powder," yet another opium preparation to survive into the twentieth century.

❖

Laudanum and other opium-based medications just got more and more popular in Europe, until it seemed no self-respecting author or poet could call himself such unless he used it. Men like Thomas de Quincey and Samuel Taylor Coleridge were heavy users of opium, as was Edgar Allan Poe. Poems like "The Raven" are products of opium dreams—nebulous moods and fantastic images that reflect the drug's typical effects.

Charles Dickens made frequent visits to London's opium dens to research the opium-smoking murderer of his novel *Edwin Drood*. It's also a fact that Dickens used opium himself to calm his nerves before public appearances and to help him sleep, especially while traveling.

And while Arthur Conan Doyle's detective, Sherlock Holmes, was partial to morphine injections to enhance an evening's relaxation, the villains in his stories were big opium consumers—usually smoking it just like the heathen Chinese.

Opium was so popular among Romantic-era poets that it soon became vogue to deny one's use and accuse rivals of "cheating"—using opium to beef up otherwise feeble imaginations. E.B. Browning was an opium user, who was accused of cheating with opium and Samuel Taylor Coleridge (who penned his famous poem "Kubla Khan" after awaking from an opium dream) sniped that de Quincey's works were fraudulently created by laudanum.

De Quincey responded by declaring himself "the pope of the true church of opium." It's not a bad title, considering how his *Confessions of An English Opium-Eater* (and other works dedicated to the drug) inspired generations of aspiring poets to follow in his footsteps and slug down some laudanum. While de Quincey reveled in his opium use, Coleridge spent much of his life fighting against his opium habit.

In a world a century away from even aspirin, where almost any illness was potentially fatal and always debilitating and painful, opium was seen as a purely Good Thing. Society had not yet learned negative opinions about habitual non-medicinal use of opium. Such a concept would probably have been more than a little nonsensical. The very fact that someone felt bad unless he took opium indicated a legitimate need for it. In fact, Coleridge himself recounted an anecdote where a child, after hearing him go on and on about how horrible he felt without his opium, asked him why, if life was so terrible without laudanum, why didn't he just take some and be his old self?

Although Coleridge had taken opium for various purposes for more than ten years, he didn't seem to have any inner conflicts about it until he was hit with nasty kidney infections that forced him to use large doses of laudanum for a lengthy period of time. Following his illness, the poet discovered he felt like shit if he didn't take his doses. Coleridge tried repeatedly to kick cold turkey... and failed in a pool of sweat and vomit. He tried to reduce his dose, enduring whatever bone-aching pain came with it until he got sick again and needed it. He then spent his days trying not to take opium.

In the end Coleridge never did shake off his need for opium, but he did succeed in his efforts to demonize it.

It is men like Coleridge who helped transmogrify opium from a simple commodity to a concrete example of an evil so great it required the most draconian measures to control it. And like the prohibitionists he inspired, his arrogance matched his hypocrisy. As early as 1808, Coleridge vowed to a friend that "If I ever entirely recover," he would consider it his "sacred duty" to anonymously publish his "Case," to save the hordes of lowbrow workers caught in the thrall of opium.

"The practice of taking opium is dreadfully spread," he wrote, "all among the labouring classes." Coleridge liked to recount his visits to druggists, quizzing them about how much opium they sold, then gasp at the idea of so much opium being freely sold to the low-class worker brutes. And he proclaimed, "surely this demands legislative interference!"

Meanwhile, Coleridge's self-hatred and love of opium set a tone to be aped by generations of prohibitionist elitists. But Coleridge didn't always hate opium. For at least a decade, the bard couldn't praise it enough. In a letter to his brother (and fellow opium enthusiast), he wrote how laudanum gave him "repose, not sleep: but YOU, I believe, know how divine that repose is—what a spot of enchantment, a green spot of fountains, & flowers & trees, in the very heart of a waste of Sands!" Coleridge said taking opium raised his intellect, "spiritualized" it even. He felt as if he could float around in the air, carried by this magic breeze, "along an infinite ocean cradled in the flower of the Lotos."

And of course there was that late autumn day in 1797 when Coleridge knocked back two grains of opium (approximately 130 mgs.) and nodded off on a journey to his own private Xanadu. When he awoke he wrote down part of what he'd seen in the unfinished poem "Kubla Khan":

> *And all who heard should see them there,*
> *And all should cry, Beware! Beware!*
> *His flashing eyes, his floating hair!*
> *Weave a circle round him thrice*
> *And close your eyes with holy dread,*
> *For he on honey-dew hath fed,*
> *And drunk the milk of Paradise.*

WHAT OPIUM FEELS LIKE

ANCIENT GREEKS CALLED IT "DESTROYER OF GRIEF" BECAUSE OPIUM NOT only frees a person from physical agony, it releases him from psychic pain as well. Even today in many places in the Middle East, chilled glasses of poppy tea are traditionally served to guests at funerals to ease their sorrow.

Sumerians called poppies "plants of joy" because of the euphoria they bring. But poppy euphoria is very different from the euphoria produced by laughing gas, alcohol or amphetamines. Opium euphoria is gentler and not at all boisterous. It is not the delirious euphoria of barbiturates or alcohol.

Opium is the mother of all analgesics—there is not much pain that can withstand the effects of opium. Its isolated alkaloids and the semi-synthetic drugs derived from them have proven so remarkable that scientists have returned to opium again and again in attempts to learn its secrets. Such investigation has led to milestones in the study of endogenous chemicals and their various receptors controlling pain, mood, sex and growth hormones, and even the immune system.

As a recreational drug it is both energizing and calming. Opium stimulates the higher brain functions of the cerebral cortex, even as it depresses the central nervous system. The effects of opium are fairly predictable, running along a continuum of feelings roughly corresponding to dose, but certain features are always present in an opium high.

Small doses produce a sense of well-being and relaxation. Opium is so effective at relieving tension that this is why it was so commonly used in patent medicines for maladies called "nervous ailments." Indeed, the word "tranquilizer" was first coined to describe opium. Today opiate use for anxiety has been superseded by tranquilizing drugs such as Valium or other benzodiazepines.

But opium's relaxation is not particularly soporific or hypnotic. The sleep it produces is not deep and for all the talk of "opium dreams," there is evidence that opium suppresses the REM stage of sleep normally associated with dreaming. For this reason it's better to consider these dreams as a form of hallucination.

The difficulty in describing the sometimes fantastic opium dreams is expressed by Walter Colron, an American who slugged down a large dose of opium after reading de Quincey's famous *Confessions*.

After his dose took effect he "lapsed into a disturbed slumber," he recalled, "in which it appeared to me that I retained my consciousness entire, while visions passed before me which no language can convey and no symbols of happiness or terror represent." That's too bad, because his subsequent dream was a rollercoaster of flying so close to heaven he could hear the Aristotelian "music of the spheres" before he fell from the sky, caromed off a thundercloud, got caught in a river's torrent, and was shot out into the ocean, where waves marshaled themselves into a physical representation of the baseline of a "world anthem." And all this happened before he witnessed the dying Pole Star, bending planets, and a black hole of exhausted worlds and unspeakable gloom before the huge serpents and the icebergs, prior to freezing and sinking to the ocean floor, where a mermaid warmed him back to life.

In 1842, William Blair wrote of his experiences with opium for a New York magazine. He does as good a job as anyone in describing the first flush of opium and its poetic effects on perception.

> While I was sitting at tea, I felt a strange sensation, totally unlike any thing I had ever felt before; a gradual creeping thrill, which in a few minutes occupied every part of my body, lulling to sleep the before-mentioned racking pain, producing a pleasing glow from head to foot, and inducing a sensation of dreamy exhilaration (if the phrase be intelligible to others as it is to me), similar in nature but not in degree to the drowsiness caused by wine, though not inclining me to sleep; in fact so far from it, that I longed to engage in some active exercise; to sing, dance, or leap.

For amusement he went to a play where "so vividly did I feel my vitality—for in this state of delicious exhilaration even mere excitement seemed absolute elysium—that I could not resist the temptation to break out in the strangest vagaries, until my companions thought me deranged."

After clowning around for a bit Blair took his seat and literally took in the play.

> After I had been seated a few minutes, the nature of the excitement changed, and a "waking sleep" succeeded. The actors on the stage vanished; the stage itself lost its reality; and before my entranced sight

magnificent halls stretched out in endless succession with gallery above gallery, while the roof was blazing with gems, like stars whose rays alone illumined the whole building, which was thronged with strange, gigantic figures, like the wild possessors of a lost globe ... I will not attempt farther to describe the magnificent vision which a little pill of "brown gum" had conjured up from the realm of ideal being. No words that I can command would do justice to its Titanian splendor and immensity.

As the dose of opium increases, relaxation and contentedness become even more blissful and euphoric. The kind of quasi-hallucinations Blair refers to are common but in no way similar to the harsh and powerful hallucinations brought on by psychedelic drugs like LSD. The visions are gentle, dreamlike and do not dominate the experience. Opium hallucinations are more an addition to reality rather than an intrusion, and such hallucinations vanish upon direct attention.

The same goes for visual images. People report animals from squirrels to tigers being present in the room with them. Nearly always the animals are harmless and cause no alarm, only interest. But should you try to touch them, or to scrutinize the hallucination too carefully, the vision melts away just as a dream. More opium increases the blending of thought, dream, and reality.

Another famous opium fan was the movie star Errol Flynn, who wrote of his drug experiences in his 1960 autobiography *My Wicked, Wicked Ways*. Here he gives us an account of an opium high, along with something of the flavor of a real-life opium den. Guided by a beautiful Chinese girl named Ting Ling, Flynn finds himself smack in the middle of an early American opium den:

I entered and was confronted with a dark blue haze and a curious odour. There were only two people here. Sure enough they were on their elbows. The blue haze seemed to hang over them.
I sat on a soft mat. Ting Ling sat beside me.

A man entered the room with an orange that was cut in half and a lamp which was half copper, half jade. He scooped out the pulp interior of the orange and bored four little portholes into it. I watched Ting Ling while this operation was being done. Her eyes were wider as she looked at the little lamp.

A tiny flame was put in the empty half-orange.

The man also had what looked like a tin of English tobacco.

In Chinese Ting Ling had a long debate with him. I figured she was fixing the price.

Quickly a round wooden pillow was put near me. "Lie on your elbow," she panted. "Lie down. Relax."

Ting Ling arranged the pillow with a little impatient gesture, and I was made more or less comfortable.

She herself sat cross-legged, that blue haze around her, like a goddess, enchanted, distant, close, mysterious, all things.

The attendant took out two instruments like crochet needles. He opened the tin box and removed a black treacly substance—opium in the raw.

Ting Ling looked down at it carefully, nodded brightly. "Very good stuff. Very good."

Sitting cross-legged, the attendant cooked this inside the orange and the flame. It bubbled. He mashed it skillfully, delicately, like an artisan.

My eyes followed the work, fascinated.

Here he produced a magnificent instrument. It looked like an early saxophone, but small at each end.

Ting Ling took the freshly prepared pill from the attendant and put it in the end of the piccolo-like instrument, jamming it in.

She inhaled and held.

I counted. It was a long time.

Very slowly she exhaled.

She puffed very strongly, sibilantly inhaling. In a most truly graceful way she lay down beside me.

Silence.

She lay there staring into the ceiling—that lovely neck, beautiful face. Her figure writhed a little beside me on the mat.

After a time she slowly turned to me on her left elbow. "Now, darling"— the first time she had ever called me that — "your turn. You see what I do?"

Surprisingly she lapsed in a pidgin English. "You do same. All same."

I grabbed the instrument and drew on it. The taste was unlike any tobacco that I ever had but not unpleasant. Certainly it wasn't burning my throat in any way.

The man prepared another little round black pill, stuck it on the end of the crochet needle and put it inside the orange. I tried to hold it and go through the same motions as Ting Ling had done.

She seemed to be looking at me with a far-away amusement. "Do you feel anything?" she asked.

"No." I didn't, except that I had a feeling I'd like to open the window.

"All right. Finish that one. Then lie down."

Together we lay side by side, both staring at the ceiling.

Suddenly that ceiling seemed to take on a new dimension. I felt Ting Ling's little hand on my right wrist. "How you feel?"

"Fine."

"You take a little bit more."

She said something in a soft tone to the fellow who prepared the smokes. He prepared another little pill.

The half-orange had grown bigger. Somehow, I don't know, but it seemed that it should be hanging from the ceiling like a Chinese lantern and my eyes were glued to it, fascinated.

I took the next umchuck, as Ting Ling told me it was pronounced in Macao.

Lying back, I began to feel a sense of panic. The orange in front of me was no longer an orange. It was a big old lantern, but it was now hilariously funny, because it was doing a dance and smiling at me.

Next thing my mind was clear as a crystal and I saw things as I have never seen them in sober perspective.

My life came before me.

It made sense.

There was this beauty beside me, looking into my eyes with what I believed was true tenderness, even passion.

I stroked her.

A lethargy came over me.

My body came out of my body. There I was on the floor, facing Ting Ling. It was extraordinary how my other body—I had two— hovered above me looking down. There was Flynn, four feet over my head, floating, held by invisible strands of I don't know what, a thing ethereal, bodiless, motionless, relaxed, amused by the whole façade and procession of his life.

Here was my love of my life by my side; so now we were three.

I whispered in Ting Ling's ear with what I can only suppose was the most stupid giggle. "Darling, darling, don't I look strange?"

She looked at me.

I said, "No no. Me, up there."

She looked up and a strange smile crossed her lips. She said, "Put your head back. Dream."

I did.

I don't know how long it was I led a completely dual life, the one above me watching everything I did.

I was quite in charge of my limbs. As a matter of fact I seemed to have the strength of four men, let alone two.

When I took Ting Ling to another room I had never known I was capable of such feats.

Today I'm told that the effect of opiates removes sexual desire in the man in inverse ratio to the female, who becomes more excited. Dr. Flynn can tell you that such is not the case.

I made love to Ting Ling in ways and manners that I would never believe myself capable of.

POPULAR PERCEPTIONS OF OPIUM

FOR CENTURIES, OPIUM WAS ONE OF THE FEW EFFECTIVE MEDICINES IN A doctor's bag. As newer medicines such as aspirin, chlorals, and barbiturates were introduced, opium began to be seen as old-fashioned. Strangely enough, opium itself, in the form of some of its refined components like morphine and codeine, also helped push out the general use of opium in medicine. Eventually opium became known as a drug used only by devious Chinese people, urban scum, urbane flappers and stars of Hollywood.

Every town of any size in the Wild West had its opium dens where opium and women were available to the dusty cowboys.

One of Thomas Edison's first movies was entitled *The Opium Smoker* and it treated the proto-moviegoer with a look inside one of the fabled opium dens, rumored to be in every city—traps for morally upright white girls especially. The opium den still evokes a powerful image today, serving as the archetypal "den of iniquity."

Leering villains and innocent teenage prey were not the only ones to become enamored of the juice of the poppy in those days. Many famous writers and artists used opium regularly as did the common folks. The upper crust made the distinction that opium's effects depended upon class or race. Laborers and Chinese people were believed to be more adversely affected by opium. Not so the movers and shakers. The wealthy were particularly fond of drinking laudanum, or spending a pleasant afternoon sucking on opium or even morphine throat lozenges. Winston Churchill was particularly partial to preparations containing heroin, according to family pharmacy records.

Poor slobs trapped in Industrial-era sweatshops used opium only when they could not afford gin—interesting considering that opium is cheaper, healthier and doesn't cause fights or hangovers. A night's drinking could easily bankrupt one of these wage slaves, so opium was a staple. It was used even more by women who were excluded from public bars, or by children for almost any reason, but primarily to bring on sleep or, tragically, to keep them immobile while mom went to slave beside her husband in the factory.

❖

In America, perhaps a good tenth of the population was addicted to opium, and a higher percentage were frequent users. Figures of the exact number of addicts are difficult to determine because addiction had yet to acquire the political significance it has now. Numbers of addicts are deduced from the amount of opium consumption per capita, which was then a perfectly legal drug. In the 1890s, when opium use is believed to have reached its peak, the U.S. was importing more than 52 grains (330 mgs) per person per year. In 1883, the wholesome farm folk of Iowa supported 3,000 drugstores selling opiate concoctions. Historian David Musto estimates there were about a quarter of a million addicts in the U.S. at a time when the entire population was pegged at 76 million. At that time, most of these opium addicts were middle-class or wealthier, white women in their post-childbearing years.

At the time, opium was abundant, and sold by the pound in grocery stores and was used in about one-third of the medicines in the eighteenth and nineteenth centuries. Today, tranquilizers and synthetic painkillers like Demerol have largely replaced opium and its direct derivatives.

OPIUM AS A GIFT OF GOD

MANY PHYSICIANS OF PAST CENTURIES CONSIDERED OPIUM DIVINE IN origin. A plant capable of such miraculous deeds seemed supernatural. Today, the belief persists because of some startling similarities between opium and chemicals produced in the human body.

The effects of opium are closely related to a number of brain chemicals known collectively as endorphins, which stimulate different areas of the brain known as endorphin receptors. All vertebrates (and some invertebrates) share the same system of endorphin receptors in essentially the same parts of the brain and in the same concentrations. Seawater has roughly the same salinity as human blood and the earth's surface is covered by about two-thirds water—the same proportion that makes up each cell in the human body. From what we know of the evolution of the human brain, it is clear that this system of opioid chemicals has been with our species for a long time and is at least as important for the survival of our species as our ability to manufacture antibodies or blood cells.

Opium's chemical structure is so astonishingly similar to chemicals we need to survive, it seems impossible that it could be a coincidence. That the poppy contains opium is as miraculous as slicing open an exotic fruit and using its juice as a substitute for blood.

The body's own version of opium—endorphins—is not a single entity and neither is opium. Morphine may appear to be the most important constituent of opium, but that is a gross simplification. Opium could not be what it is without morphine but to ascribe its powers to this single alkaloid is like saying blood's most crucial ingredient is water. You could make that argument—dry blood would be pretty useless, after all—but it falls far short of accounting for blood or its functions.

The emphasis science puts on morphine (and its chemical cousins) has obscured the true nature of opium. Today the Western world prefers its own, more "miraculous" products of high technology. To the world today, poppies have become forbidden fruit, linked in the public mind with illegal drugs only.

The following poem was written in England just after the first laws restricting opium were enacted (but left the British opium business free to feed as much as possible to China). In it, the poet laments that he didn't learn to like alcohol, which is exempt from laws designed to protect the public health and welfare.

OPIUM EATER'S SOLILOQUY

I'd been cheered up, at my chandoo-shop, for years at
    least two-score,
To perform my daily labour, and was never sick or sore,
But they said this must not be;
So they've passed a stern decree,
And they've made my chandoo-seller shut his hospitable door.

If I'd only cultivated, now, a taste for beer and gin,
Or had learnt at pool or baccarat my neighbour's coin to win,
I could roam abroad o' nights,
And indulge in these delights,
And my soul would not be stigmatized, as being steeped in sin.

But mine's a heathen weakness for a creature-comfort far
Less pernicious than their alcohol, more clean than their cigar,
They have sent their howlings forth
From their platform in the North,
And 'twixt me and my poor pleasure have opposed a righteous bar.

—Sir Patrick Hehir, M.D.
London, 1894

MORE OPIATED PHYSICAL EFFECTS

OPIUM DOES NOT CAUSE THE LOSS OF JUDGMENT THAT ALCOHOL IS SO infamous for. In place of giddy stumbling, there is "emotional and intellectual elevation and increased muscular energy, and the capacity to act and bear fatigue is greatly augmented," according to Dr. George Wood, a University of Pennsylvania medical professor, in 1888.

His last observation is why opium was and is still used by those engaged in heavy labor. Opium also increases their stamina and resistance to boredom. The overwhelming drudgery of a sharecropper or deckhand would be unbearable without the drug. Chinese coolies of the last century and many Indian laborers today find that a morning dose of opium is essential for performing the hard work of poverty. Another dose in the evening serves to ease the pain of aching muscles and any other misery.

Opium smokers typically take the drug in this twice-a-day fashion. The amount of opium needed by any particular user tends to rise and fall in response to outside factors such as stress. Although a user's needs will almost invariably climb at first, eventually a standard dose will establish itself.

In many ways, opium is self-regulating. At a certain point a person will get sick to his stomach or simply fall asleep if he eats or smokes too much of it.

The best-known effects of opium are pain relief and control of even the worst diarrhea. As opiate receptors load up, fear and anxiety disappear, and the patient feels detached from discomfort. This feeling of detachment is the most important feature of opiate analgesia. As a deadening agent, opium has almost no effect. If measured purely for its ability to alleviate the sensation of pain, morphine, opium, or any of the others would score no better than aspirin. It is the perception of pain that opium alters, and that makes all the difference in the world.

It's as if the pain were happening to someone else or to no one at all.

Pain is not perceived or experienced as uncomfortable. This, together with the erasure of anxiety or fear of coming pain, is how opium (and opiate or opioid drugs) eradicate the torture of multiple bone fractures or torn flesh. It is why no pain-wracked patient, and especially no one with a terminal but excruciatingly painful illness, ever needs to feel pain at all. Morphine, opium, heroin, or any of the other variations on the theme can all be used to render pain irrelevant.

Other physical effects of opium are constricted pupils and itching, especially on the nose. Interestingly, there is no tolerance to pupil constriction—it happens to every user every time. The itching feeling is not unpleasant. Although you can relieve it by taking an antihistamine, most people find they enjoy it and you'll find opium users blissfully rubbing and scratching their faces. The itch is not strong, nor is it irritating so there isn't any temptation to scratch to the point of injury.

Opiates also paralyze the bowel, which can ease stomach cramps and also cause constipation. In most people this doesn't cause any problem or if it does, it can be remedied by the use of a laxative. Stories of severe intestinal impaction are told but such cases are rare and normally associated with some of the stronger, synthetic opiates, or with the use of just one of opium's alkaloids, such as codeine—not opium.

Another effect is difficulty in urinating, especially in starting the flow of pee. Some people can take care of this by tickling their buttocks with their fingertips.

Sweating, too, is a common effect of opiate use and even continues after use is stopped. This is also one of its therapeutic features and opium mixed with ipecac used to be prescribed as a sudorific—sweat-inducer. Like itching, this is thought to be partially a result of histamine release. It's also probably associated with the effects opiates have on the endocrine system and body temperature regulation.

Opium and opiates lower blood pressure, but some individual components have a more pronounced effect than others (i.e. papaverine, which has been used for exactly this effect). Another opium alkaloid, protopine, can lower blood pressure or raise it, depending on the dosage. Even though some people may experience heartburn after taking opiates, opium and opiates reduce acid production in the stomach. The heartburn comes as a result of the relaxation of muscle tone (tension) in the esophagus, which allows acid to be splashed up into the throat—a condition known as "acid reflux." This is the same reaction that reduces peristalsis in the intestine and slows the action of the digestive system. In large amounts, opiates can even make swallowing more difficult.

And, of course, coughing is quickly controlled by lots of opiates, codeine being the one most favored for this purpose, although heroin was originally marketed and used for this effect.

The most dangerous effect of opiates is their depression of respiration. Morphine, especially, causes breathing to slow down as individual breaths get shallower. This happens because opiates interfere with the way the brain responds to carbon dioxide levels in the blood; the user doesn't feel uncomfortable even if the drug is taken in sufficient quantities to halt breathing altogether. This is how people die of overdoses of heroin, morphine, or other opiates. It can happen with opium, too, but it's a far greater problem with morphine alone. On the other hand, some opiates exhibit very powerful painkilling properties with only a fraction of the respiratory depression.

In some users, nausea is a common side effect. In fact, it's a typical response to a heroin user's first use or two. Tolerance to nausea usually resolves this problem in short order, but not always. There are many opiate users who continue to throw up every time they use their drugs, even years down the line. This not only gives an idea of how good dope must feel to them, it also reveals another characteristic about this kind of nausea: it's not as intense as the nausea and vomiting that accompany, say, food poisoning. Some people have described it as more akin to coughing than anything else.

Although the exact mechanism for this vomiting isn't known, it's thought to be vestibular in nature—that is, it has to do with the inner ear. One way to relieve the nausea of opiates (about 80% of the time) is to lie on your back and stay still for a while. After ten or twenty minutes, this nausea should depart.

The stereotypical opiate user has a real sweet tooth. Opiates affect the way the body uses sugar, specifically glucose, and some study is being given to watching how the brain utilizes glucose (its primary source of energy) while its opiate receptors are antagonized by endorphins or drugs like morphine. Already it has been demonstrated that there is a link between the body's opioid system and the palatability of certain foods.

As mentioned earlier, opium can lower blood sugar, which might be fine for diabetics, but can set off cravings for sugar in non-diabetics. Studies support this stereotype, showing opiate users consume far more sugar and carbohydrates as a portion of their total daily caloric intake than non-users, although their total intake of calories is the same. Of course if a poor person uses most of his money to buy drugs, cutting back on food to do it he will lose weight and become malnourished. Opiates are also known for their appetite-suppressing qualities.

But another factor involved is the opium user's reduced need for protein. A heroin addict may require only about half the protein in his diet than non-drug users. This is thought to be a result of his body's shutdown of endorphin production, which uses proteins as its raw material, the source of amino acids that endorphins are made from. If this is true, it shows how truly essential endorphins are to the human organism considering that half of the most difficult to obtain nutrients are turned over to their production. ❖

CHAPTER 2
THE WAR ON POPPIES

So long as we have failed to eliminate any of the causes of human despair, we do not have the right to try to eliminate those means by which man tries to cleanse himself of despair.

— Antonin Artaud —

General Security: The Liquidation of Opium

THOMAS JEFFERSON WAS A DRUG CRIMINAL. BUT HE MANaged to escape the terrible sword of justice by dying a century before the DEA was created. In 1987 agents from the Drug Enforcement Agency showed up at Monticello, Jefferson's famous estate.

Jefferson had planted opium poppies in his medicinal garden, and opium poppies are now deemed illegal. Now, the trouble was the folks at the Monticello Foundation, which preserves and maintains the historic site, were discovered flagrantly continuing Jefferson's crimes.

The agents were blunt: The poppies had to be immediately uprooted and destroyed or else they were going to start making arrests, and Monticello Foundation personnel would perhaps face lengthy stretches in prison.

The story sounds stupid now, but it scared the hell out of the people at Monticello, who immediately started yanking the forbidden plants. A DEA man noticed the store was selling packets of "Thomas Jefferson's Monticello Poppies." The seeds had to go, too. While poppy seeds might be legal, it is never legal to plant them. Not for any reason.

Employees even gathered the store's souvenir T-shirts—with silkscreened photos of Monticello poppies on the chest—and burned them. Nobody told them to do this, but, under the circumstances, no one dared risk the threat.

Jefferson's poppies are gone without a trace now. Nobody said much at the time, nor are they saying much now. Visitors to Monticello don't learn how the Founding Father cultivated poppies for their opium. His personal opium use and poppy cultivation may as well never have happened.

The American War on Drugs started with opium and it continues today. Deception is key to this kind of social control, along with the usual threats of mayhem. Ever since the passage of the Harrison Act made opium America's first "illicit substance" in 1914, propaganda has proven itself most effective in the war on poppies. This has not been done so much by eradicating the poppy plant from the nation's soil as by eradicating the poppy from the nation's mind.

Prosecutions for crimes involving opium or opium poppies are rare. But that has less to do with the frequency of poppy crimes and everything to do with suppressing information about the opium poppy. A public trial might inadvertently publicize forbidden information at odds with the common spin about poppies and opium. This might pique interest in the taboo subject and, worse, undermine faith in the government.

The U.S. government strategy to create and enforce deliberate ignorance about opium, opium poppies, and everything connected with them has proven remarkably effective. The Monticello campaign exemplifies an effective tactic. The poppies were swiftly removed, and *sotto voce* threats ensured no one would talk about it afterward. Today, visitors to Monticello learn nothing about opium poppy cultivation or why Jefferson cultivated it in his garden.

Disinformation about poppies has been spread far and wide. Some of it is subtle, like when the *New York Times* talks about people growing "heroin poppies." Some misinformation is so bald-faced as to stun the listener into silence, as when a DEA agent tells a reporter that the process of getting opium from opium poppies is so complex and dangerous that "I don't even think a person with a Ph.D. could do it."

This enforced ignorance reduces the chances of anyone even accidentally discovering the truth about poppies. Poring through back issues of pharmaceutical industry news from Tasmania might yield a mother load of cutting edge poppy science—from genetically altered poppies that ooze double-strength opium to state-of-the-art machines designed to manufacture "poppy straw concentrate." Tasmania's output meets roughly a third of the world's narcotic requirement. But how many people know that Tasmania is the home of the world's largest and most modern opium industry?

✤

Opium and opium poppy ignorance is augmented by widespread false beliefs, chief among them that it is extremely difficult for opium poppies to grow anywhere in the United States. Opium poppies surely require exotic climates or special climatic conditions, don't they? They're found on remote mountainsides in the Golden Triangle and Afghanistan, where growing them is a secret art known only to a few indigenous people who jealously guard the seeds from hostile competitors.

These beliefs are all widely held, but entirely untrue. Opium poppies, in fact, grow nearly everywhere but the North and South Poles.

The second prong of the strategy is the copious propaganda that demonizes opium, opium poppies and opiates. At times this demonization has been brazenly racist, catering to the xenophobic American mind at the beginning of the twentieth century. Later propaganda linked opium with the despised German "Hun" who ate babies and (as was reported) had been mixing narcotics into children's candy and women's face powder in a diabolical plot to weaken the nation from the inside. Later, Germans were replaced by communists, who also shipped narcotics to America's youth to weaken and enslave us. This was the authoritative word from Harry Anslinger, the infamous first Commissioner of the Federal Bureau of Narcotics.

Another example of false history is the mythical "soldier's disease" or "army disease" that supposedly plagued the land after the Civil War. According to the story, opium and morphine were used so extensively during the war as a painkiller for wounded soldiers (especially amputees) that the inevitable result was opium and morphine addiction. As a result, crowds of broken-down men roamed the countryside, ramming themselves full of holes with their crude syringes, having been turned into dope slaves by the good intentions of doctors.

This perfect example of anti-drug propaganda sounds plausible enough that few ever question it. And it has endured long after researchers discovered that this mythical legend was purely invention. There is no documentation of any mass opiate addiction after the Civil War. The term "soldier's disease" or its variants did not appear in literature until decades later. Yet the story fits the officially approved stereotype by portraying opium and morphine as so powerful and addictive that they could rob anyone's soul.

If you knew that opium poppies do not grow in the U.S., you would not recognize an opium poppy even if you were staring directly at it. So, the idea of making opium tea from a bunch of dried decorative flowers purchased at K-Mart is ridiculous—absurd, really. If it were that easy, wouldn't everyone be doing it?

Perhaps. But the establishment prefers to not test it. The idea of an individual having control over one's own life, especially regarding pain relief, is far too democratic to be embraced by tyrants.

The government and its allies in the narco-military complex have gone to great lengths to set things up as they are, and not allow a shift in control would affect licit or illicit sales of narcotics, poppy seeds, and any products derived from *Papaver somniferum*. In a market the size of America, nothing is too insignificant to generate huge sums of money. And the opium poppy is hardly insignificant.

JUST HOW IMPORTANT IS THE OPIUM POPPY, ANYWAY?

IN AN ECONOMY THAT CAN SUPPORT COMPETING BRANDS OF KIWI JUICE, it is instructive to consider the humble poppy seed. A half-gram of them dotting the top of a bagel gets multiplied in a hurry. Americans consume tons of poppy seed, all of it imported, and much of it from Tasmania.

Of course, the poppy's most important product is narcotic drugs. They are the only drugs that can adequately control severe pain. They do a bang-up job on mild and moderate pain, too, but the severe pain of a gunshot wound, burns, post-operative and various cancer pains can be relieved only by opioid drugs. Without these drugs, modern medicine, and modern warfare, would be impossible. That is to say, modern civilization could not exist without them.

Demand for the morphine and other alkaloids found in opium is what economists call "inelastic." There is no other source for morphine, codeine, or any of the other opiates used to control pain. Another opium alkaloid, papaverine, is the precursor for several cardiac medications and can also be used by itself as a cardiac medication. Of course, "inelastic" is something of an understatement when describing the intense demand created by the nation's heroin users and the billion-dollar industry they support. Technological advances have failed to match the poppy when it comes to making narcotics.

The total synthesis of morphine was not accomplished until 1852—codeine would take another 30 years—and it did little more than confirm the molecular structure. There are synthetic opioids that do not require morphine or any other poppy alkaloid to manufacture, but most synthetics have pharmacological problems that make them inferior choices as medicine, and all of them lack morphine's nearly 200-year record of safety and efficacy. Synthetics, like methadone or meperidine

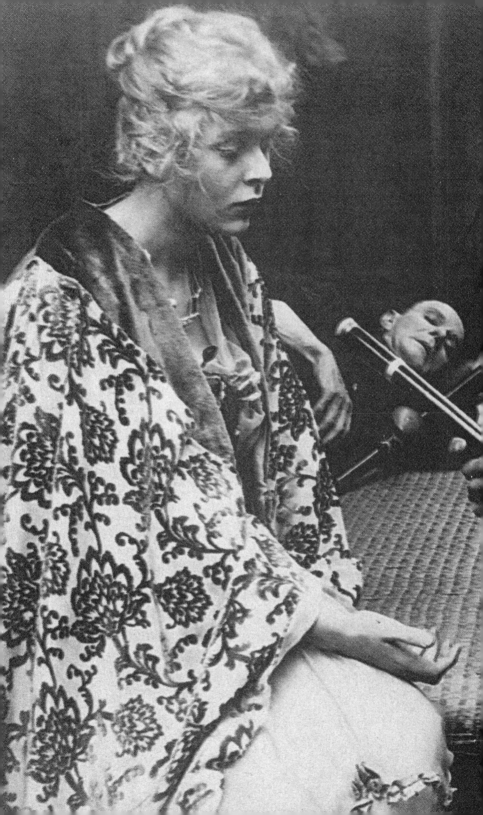

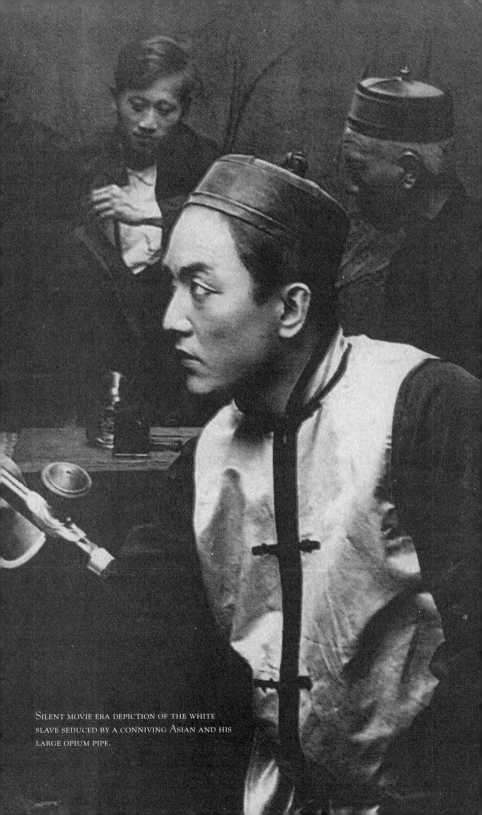

SILENT MOVIE ERA DEPICTION OF THE WHITE
SLAVE SEDUCED BY A CONNIVING ASIAN AND HIS
LARGE OPIUM PIPE.

(Demerol) are expensive to make, requiring specialized equipment and skilled workers. A few acres of land and a single farmer can produce far more and better narcotic material than the most efficient drug factory— at a fraction of the cost.

❖

Understanding the history of opium in America is an exercise in discerning fact from fiction.

Once the lies are exposed it becomes possible to evaluate the results of enforcing ignorance on the population. An examination of the truth is its own reward of course, especially considering opium poppies.

Critical thinking about opium, poppies or poppy seeds is actively discouraged. Though it is widely known that eating poppy seeds will give a positive test for opiates on a urinalysis, few make the connection that this is because the poppy seeds are opium poppy seeds. Even when the connection is made, it is common to assume (incorrectly) that the poppy seeds have been sterilized or come from an opium poppy variety that produces little or no "dope."

And most people are surprised to learn that the opium poppy can be grown anywhere in the United States. In the 1930s, the barely-hatched Bureau of Narcotics surveilled the kitchen gardens of Czech immigrants growing poppies in Minnesota! Minnesota is a land of open plains and no exotic remote mountainsides, and their winters are unlike anything in the tropics.

The truth is: there is no state where the poppy cannot grow. There is probably no state where opium poppies are not growing right now. The U.S. government itself has grown poppies in such diverse states as Montana, Arizona, Maryland, and Washington.

The seeds on sale in grocery stores are indeed opium poppy seeds, which are more than 90% viable. And chances are very good that they come from poppy cultivars that produce some of the strongest opium in the world! Good seeds equal good opium. No one has yet found a way to breed the poppy to produce more and better seeds without also making

OPIUM GETS IN UNDER FALSE PRETENSES

PROPAGANDA FROM THE 1930S SHOWING HOW OUR FRIEND THE OPIUM POPPY
SLIPS PAST CUSTOMS.

more and better morphine (and other alkaloids) in the opium. In the future, perhaps the government will mandate that seeds be sterilized, or they might mandate that we use seeds from some other poppy with edible seed. That is thankfully doubtful, though, and not just because the seeds would have a different taste.

❖

For a time in the 1970s there was talk of growing the so-called "safer poppy"—*Papaver bracteatum*. This species does not manufacture morphine, it is said. But it produces thebaine, similar to morphine in structure but without any of the sought-after effects. Its real value is as starting material for some of the most potent semi-synthetic opiates available. Dilaudid is one of them.

The program never got off the ground. A few test plots were planted, and there was a lot of talk at meetings, but, in the end, the DEA withdrew its original support for the idea then killed it. Perhaps it was a fear that *Papaver bracteatum* might hybridize with *P. somniferum* or otherwise begin producing morphine. Or perhaps it was killed because *P. bracteatum*, like a number of other Papaver species, has been known to produce morphine.

The Jaws of Death

A slinking thing with hellish sting,
The reptile known as Dope,
Its poison breath is living death
Beyond the pale of hope,
And in the blight of endless night
Its countless victims grope.

In stricken homes the reptile roams
On hearthstones bare and bleak.
Ambition dies in youthful eyes,
Slain by the noxious reek.
For Dope is strong and prospers long
Because the laws are weak.
By George E. Phair.

Atlanta Georgian, 27 February 1935

Vigorous eradication measures like those carried out against marijuana are not possible with poppies. Such measures are too high-profile and would call attention to the poppy. Unlike cannabis growing in ditches or in plots, this flower is most commonly cultivated in gardens all over the country—a favorite of decorators and little old ladies. Targeting these people for poison spray might not be such good PR.

THE POPPY REBELLION

WE REMEMBER THE "POPPY REBELLION" OF THE 1940S, STAGED BY CALIfornia farmers trying to increase their earnings by domestically producing the poppy seeds whose import had been cut off by the war. Prices had risen manifold, to around 50 cents a bushel, representing opportunities for profit among American citizens.

By this time the federal government had cajoled and threatened every other farmer in the country, even going so far as to dictate the editorial policy of Oregon and Washington newspapers by suppressing poppy information and painting those farmers who insisted on growing the crop as just this side of traitorous.

In a unanimous vote, a three-judge panel certified the Anti-Opium Poppy Act of 1942 as constitutional inasmuch as it was explicitly grounded in the treaty-making powers of the executive branch, which took precedence over all other laws in the country. This law was not repealed until the introduction of the Uniform Controlled Substances Act of 1970.

There is a tacit policy of not enforcing the laws against opium poppies. "We're not going into grandma's garden and start taking samples," reassures an anonymous DEA agent in Seattle. His counterpart at the DEA's Indianapolis office said he had not the slightest interest in poppies grown in someone's flower garden.

"We wouldn't even walk around the corner for that," he sniffed. As recently as 1996, officials of the DEA have admitted in public that the agency had a general policy of non-enforcement of the poppy laws preferring "voluntary cooperation" from within the community.

Although there is always the tacit threat of prosecution, the truth is that anything beyond a warning is fairly remarkable. Even when Customs targeted for intensive inspection of nearly every package from certain foreign countries in an operation called "Opium Blitz," the goal was not to fill jail cells. Such efforts are normally meant to send discrete and focused messages to a specific group—generally immigrants from opium-using areas of the world. Recipients of the opium are contacted (usually when they come to pick up their packages) and told, in essence, "We know you're bringing in opium; we know how you do it and why you do it, but you must stop or risk going to jail."

DRUG LORD KHUN SA'S SEAL OF APPROVAL FOR HIS GOLDEN TRIANGLE HEROIN.

In the 1980s Seattle police discovered thousands of opium poppies being deliberately cultivated by what seemed to be Hmong refugees. No arrests were made. No prosecutions were undertaken or even threatened. Later in the summer of 1997, when it was pointed out to state cops that more than a quarter-acre of opium poppies was obviously being cultivated on state land within the city of Seattle, investigators dispatched to the scene reassuringly declared that the poppies were being grown for "non-narcotic purposes," although they never said why they thought that. The poppies were not destroyed.

Looking at the statistics, it appears very difficult to get busted for poppies. Even if you are warned directly that you're doing something illegal and might end up doing time, you can call their bluff. Many have done it, but it helps if you're rich, or, at least famous. One flagrant violator is Martha Stewart, who grows opium poppies in her garden and dismisses fears about narcotics as "silly."

In response to "reports" coming out of the Northwest that people were "misusing the pods" in early 1995, the DEA launched a low-key investigation and—lo and behold—it was true! Poppies, dried and fresh, were being purchased, chopped up and pulverized, and made into a therapeutic tea. This was not the first time the practice had been discovered, though. Besides being a home remedy for many centuries throughout Europe and the rest of the world, it was once practiced by regular Joes in the United States.

Cultural references to opium poppies are curiously rare. Arguably, the most famous appears in the film *The Wizard of Oz*, when the Wicked Witch reveals her plan to use "Poppies...to make them sleepy" in order to foil the progress of Dorothy & co. Elsewhere in filmdom, poppy tea makes a cameo appearance in the original script of *Night of the Iguana* (where the brew is used to calm a distraught character). Poppy seed tea is described in the original *Casino Royale* film as an intensely pleasurable beverage with the additional (and desirable) side effect that "will blow your mind."

These few film references seem to comprise the entire extent of pop cultural impact before the surveillance state got into it. Thereafter, poppies and opium were identified as a "clear and present danger" to national security, and it was impossible to treat them with anything less than breathless concern. From the beginning of a federal "drug enforcement" agency, throughout the 1930s, 1940s, and 1950s, federal narcotics enforcers have made references to "poppy tea" and its drug use potential.

Then, as now, the "problem" was minuscule, more theoretical than real. The only time potential danger was mentioned was in support of existing or proposed laws controlling poppies in the U.S. Of course, the irony is that even as the laws forbidding poppies got ever stricter, police became increasingly hesitant to enforce any of the laws. To do so would require extensive and exceedingly obnoxious intrusions into people's lives. Because the typical poppy-grower really is a "little old lady" or other law-abiding type, it would mean—at the very least—a sustained campaign of threats against harmless citizens.

To make matters worse, for every poppy that is deliberately planted by a little old lady, there are countless others springing up as "volunteers"—products of the plant's highly evolved system of self-sowing. In this way, poppies have established themselves across the country. In Seattle, "wild" opium poppies grow through sidewalk cracks! Volunteer poppies sprout up as single plants, in groups of three, four or five, or sometimes blossom as good-sized patches anywhere that will have them. The area alongside well-drained berming that flanks the nation's interstate highways is one particularly hospitable to poppies.

SUBVERSIVE NURSERIES AND FLORISTS

TO KEEP THE STATUS QUO, THE DEA TARGETS THE KNOWLEDGE OF poppies, seeking to keep it submerged and undisseminated. To do this, agents visited nurseries and florists across the country, educating them with abrupt appearances and pointed suggestions that the proprietor pull all such stock and destroy it. Those who didn't merit a personal visit got letters written by the man in charge of the investigation. Larry Snyder is a senior DEA official working out of DEA headquarters in Washington, D.C. to quell this latest outbreak of knowledge.

A letter from Snyder was (per his request) reprinted in various trade journals and newsletters urging cooperation. This DEA intrusion into a publication's editorial policy was necessary "before this situation adds to the drug-abuse epidemic."

Florists were urged to stop selling poppies or poppy seed immediately. It did not matter how much money anyone was making off the dried ornamentals or the seeds for garden cultivation. It didn't even matter if anyone had detected criminal activity. The trade had to stop. The cops said the plant was illegal, and selling it or its seeds was a crime that could cause violators to be prosecuted. Many people called to plead with the DEA to make exceptions, at least to lighten up a bit, but they were all met with the same unyielding hard line to ditch those poppies pronto.

Something of an increase in the war had happened by summer of 1996, when a rural Georgia man was arrested for growing poppies from commercially available seeds which let the DEA draw a plausible link between the companies and the criminal. Among the potentially prosecutable seed companies was international giant Thompson & Morgan. The way in which a poor Georgia boy was targeted, as opposed to those companies, which had been previously warned, is striking.

The 32-year-old Georgia man with no criminal history, Wesley Allen Moore, lost his trailer home, young wife, and baby son. He was thrown into the Georgia prison system for two full decades without the chance of parole. An "example" was made of his case from the beginning when Georgia narcotics officers arrived at Moore's patch of scrawny poppies, shimmying down ropes from hovering helicopters. The circus surrounding his apprehension was as fundamentally mendacious as the outright lies told by the cops.

Each one of the golfball-sized seed pods on the plants could produce a kilogram of heroin, said the local sheriff, a comment that opposes the laws of physics. In truth a head will yield only a few grams of opium, of which ten percent can be expected to be morphine. Even if there were zero loss converting the morphine, the amount of diacetylmorphine (heroin) would still be measured in milligrams.

Anyone following the story in the news learned the official lies: the poppies Moore grew "could not grow in the USA and were imported," and the poppies in Grandma's yard might look identical, but they're different, they're "ornamental." The seed companies chose to ignore DEA threats. The Georgia man was crucified with a 20-year prison term, and nothing has happened to the seed companies.

THE RESULTS OF THE LATEST PROGRAM

FIVE YEARS AFTER SEED COMPANIES, FLORISTS AND NURSERIES WERE alerted to the budding "national epidemic," poppies endure and continue to grow, and their price has increased. A bunch of ten to twelve heads that could once be purchased for as little as $1.25 now cost over $10. This was to be expected when merchants realized what the new breed of flower enthusiast was willing to pay. Dried poppies are normally good sellers for dried flower merchants. Business is blooming.

Some poppy purveyors sought to placate the government by renaming their plants. The illegal *Papaver somniferum* was replaced by a "new" species that suddenly appeared. One of the most popular new species was branded *P. giganthemum*. This simple trick should fool no one. However, in an interview with a reporter for *Harper's* magazine, Larry Snyder himself extolled the virtues of this new sort of poppy. He told the reporter that he had one in his hand at that very moment. And, in his opinion, the head was larger than a *P. somniferum* head. Therefore, he didn't see why this new *P. giganthemum* species might not be considered the perfect replacement. In another disturbing display of ignorance, Snyder informed the reporter that there were some 2,500 other species of Papaver besides the demon *P. somniferum*, and he was sure that among them were even better substitutes. Actually, the number of Papaver species is estimated to be only around 250. However, his confusion is instructive. Here is the man whose career requires understanding the genesis and mechanics of a nationally threatening drug epidemic, but cannot recognize his opponent, or even understand the fundamentals of botany or plant biology. Meanwhile, his men were busy threatening citizens with prosecution for possession of a plant no one could identify, not even their superiors.

OPIUM POPPY LAW

MORE THAN 80 YEARS OF THE GOVERNMENT'S IMPOSED SILENCE REGARD-
ing poppies has done a remarkable job changing what Americans
"know" about opium and opium poppies, as well as how they feel about
them. The lies and fears surrounding opium and poppies were duly
incorporated into society's most revered alternate reality: the law.

In his article "The Historical Shift in the Perception of Opiates:
From Medicine to Social Menace"[1] J.P. Hoffmann examines the laws
prohibiting the use of opiates in the U.S. These laws, he says, were more
cause than effect with regard to public perception of the drugs:

> *Historically perceived as efficacious medicines, this perception
> has shifted to the point that contemporarily the opiates are commonly
> thought of as a social menace.*
>
> *This perception now outweighs the efficacious medicine perception
> to a substantial degree. A historical analysis indicates that this shift oc-
> curred not so much because the hazardous potential for addiction and
> overdose was discovered, nor because recreational use became wide-
> spread; rather, this shift was greatly influenced by underlying national
> economic conditions and concerns.*

Hoffman's study correctly identifies the true reasons for the suppression of opiates in the U.S. (those "national economic conditions
and concerns"), and highlights the profound effect of "authority"
on public opinion. People are reluctant to disagree with authority
figures—like doctors, religious leaders, and "statesmen," and they
find it even tougher to disagree with prevailing opinion, especially
the opinions of a peer group. Propaganda directed by President
Woodrow Wilson (who had campaigned for the office on an explicit
vow not to bring America into war) transformed a population dead

set against war into jingoistic soldiers eager to join the effort in The Great World War I.

What have been the effects of the opium ban and its resulting alterations in U.S. jurisprudence and civilization?

We can see that laws promulgated for unspoken and even hidden aims are bound to promote a perverse "justice" if they are ever applied in any fashion. They will be grossly destructive of civil liberties whenever vigorously or extensively enforced and they will promote contempt for anyone involved with law enforcement. Of course, any time the State deprives a citizen of life, property or any inalienable right by using shaky legal mechanisms, we have a situation ripe for the wholesale violation of the rights of the accused (perhaps the very heart of the Bill of Rights).

Laws enacted under false pretenses, aiming only to oppress certain people not otherwise susceptible to criminal charges, are the worst and most repulsive example of evil posing as justice. This is easily seen when the law itself is poorly understood. Poppy laws are uniformly and persistently misunderstood by the very people who write them. When cops or other government agents use force to obtain obedience to laws that they themselves cannot understand, they necessarily turn a blind eye to justice.

The way the poppy laws are written makes them impossible to understand, and the paucity of enforcement calls their legitimacy into question, as well as the sincerity or ability of those who write them. This results in the appearance of each prosecution as a textbook example of selective or malicious prosecution. Such practices are forbidden by American law and negate poppy laws a priori.

The profound ignorance of judges, cops, and lawyers tasked with upholding these laws cannot but set the stage for the imposition of rank injustice. A look at those few "poppy prosecutions" that appear in the record reveal sad tales of political repression masquerading as lofty crusades to keep the nation "pure."

THE ROLE OF PAIN IN FREEDOM

THE POPPY'S CENTRAL AND INDISPENSABLE POSITION IN OUR CIVILIZATION makes access to it important, and thus forbidding public access to the poppy is staggeringly cruel. Ceding control of opiates means ceding control of pain relief to the State... which has shown truly morbid interest in inflicting pain and denying its relief in order to effect social change and maintain social control. This is power that free people should never relinquish easily or without a fight.

To overlook the significance of pain relief would be a big mistake. Pain, after all, is the threat behind all threats, the power behind any negative reinforcement, the stick that is partner to the carrot. Pain is the archetypal "scourge of mankind." Both pain and the fear of pain make tyranny possible. Even without the participation of human evil, pain is the terrible price we pay when we violate the laws of nature.

Even the many diseases that science has "conquered" still cause severe pain. Multiple sclerosis, fibromyalgia, cancer, and burn patients often have such crippling pain that even the most powerful opiates are insufficient, and these patients long for death.

Consider also that Dr. Kevorkian once saved a patient a lifetime of hellish pain by simply agreeing to help her die. Only then did her own doctor realize the severity of her condition, that she wasn't just seeking drugs, and provide her the pain medication that he could have prescribed from the start.

And yet we are encouraged to perceive the opium poppy and its derivatives as evil. It is obvious that nature has provided for mankind an abundance of medicines to cure or treat diseases, including pain. The opium poppy does that better than the best-equipped, most dedicated scientist. Opium is easy to cultivate and miraculously useful. Opium is a blessing for the poor, wretched and oppressed.

The power to relieve pain is even greater than the power to inflict it. ✤

ENDNOTE

1. The Journal of Psychoactive Drugs 22: 53–62 (1990).

CHAPTER 3
YOUR VERY OWN POPPY TEA
(AND LAUDANUM)

Of those four winters which I passed in Indo-China opium has left the happiest memory.

— Graham Greene, *The Quiet American* —

FOR BOTH LEGAL AND SCIENTIFIC REASONS, IT'S IMPORtant to clear up confusion about the nomenclature used when describing what is sometimes called "Opium Tea." It's not "opium tea." It is "poppy tea."

Strictly speaking, you cannot make "opium tea" from poppies. Opium's legal and scientific definition describes the exuded gum from the living plant's incised seed-head. Anything else is not opium.

Poppy tea has a less precise definition but it's still pretty straightforward.

Any time you take some dried plant material, chop it up and pulverize it, brew it for a while in hot water, then strain the liquid out, you've got "tea." If you make this tea using poppies as starting material then you've got "poppy tea." If you use *Papaver somniferum* to make this poppy tea, you could call it "opium poppy tea," but then the word "opium" has more to do with the plant's name than the fresh sap exuded from its wounded seed pod.

Besides that, the identification of *Papaver somniferum* is problematic—especially when dealing with dried plants purchased at the local florist or craft shop. There are many varieties of poppy out there besides the classic opium poppy; not every poppy is *P. somniferum*.

It should be noted that getting high from tea made from dried poppies is weak evidence that the tea was made from opium poppies. There are more than 250 varieties of poppy, a great number of which contain plenty of psychoactive alkaloids besides morphine. Morphine is produced by no fewer than five species of Papaver and there are still more poppies that produce related alkaloids, some of which may have effects very similar to morphine. Poppy tea can produce effects in the drinker through other alkaloids that are metabolized into other, more active substances. This is how codeine works, for instance. And thebaine (an alkaloid found in quite a few species of Papaver) is similarly demethy-lated by the liver into oripavine. Oripavine can then be converted into still other alkaloids—including morphine.

While the effects gained from drinking a poppy tea are doubtless the most important factor for making it in the first place, it would be wrong to assume they come from opium or morphine.

Making tea from dried poppy heads is anything but new. It was a remedy in medieval Europe and it is still considered a practical, home-brewed method of treating various degrees of pain. In this country, too, poppy tea was once commonly consumed, especially by immigrants from eastern European nations. In the 1930s, agents from the newly-hatched Bureau of Narcotics conducted surveillance on Czech housewives living in Minnesota, who grew poppies for use as a medicinal tea. In 1959 the bureau's chief, Harry Anslinger, voiced his support for a continued ban on domestic cultivation of *Papaver somniferum* saying he was concerned that "dope addicts" might use home-grown opium poppies as a "rich source" of narcotics.

❖

Although opiates are some of the most strictly controlled drugs in the U.S., they remain easy and cheap to get. You don't need to smuggle opium or even grow poppies, as ample supplies of the plants are grown all over the country and not just in people's gardens. Especially in California, there are huge farms devoted to poppies (some looking quite similar to opium poppies, I must say). And smaller but no less impressive farms in Oregon and Washington and even Idaho and Montana host large poppy crops. Dried poppies are massively imported from Turkey, Holland and other countries, too, and sold in craft stores, and florists in thousands of stores nationwide—making potent, relatively low-cost opiate tea available practically everywhere. It is entirely possible that it is carried by your local grocer. It's even possible that you could walk into a grocery store and come out with all the ingredients and tools you need to make your own morphine and perhaps even heroin if you're clever.

Opium poppies are very available to the general public, commonly sold in craft stores and flower shops as bunches of dried heads. Normally these are used in floral decorations but they are still chock full of opium. Although the potency of the alkaloids is slightly reduced by drying, it remains plenty strong and can be quickly extracted by making tea from it.

The average price of dried poppies increased steadily as their popularity grew, starting in the mid-'90s. While a bunch of cellophane-wrapped poppies once went for as little as $1.25 in the early part of the decade, it's ten to 20 times that just a decade later.

It's still worth it. Don't worry too much about getting "the wrong ones" since almost every sort of round-headed poppy sold like this contains at least some worthwhile goodies.

Most of the poppies sold in stores are indeed opium poppies, *Papaver somniferum*; but there is another, sort you might come across. These poppies have smaller heads—ranging in size from about as big as a marble to slightly larger than a golf ball. The average head size is approximately the size of a small walnut. They are a dark green color when dried and are frequently full of seeds, which, like *P. somniferum*, are edible. These seeds are sometimes a brick-red color and have a smoky, nutty flavor.

Most of the poppies sold in stores are indeed opium poppies, *Papaver somniferum*; but there is another sort you might come across. These poppies have smaller heads, ranging in size from about as big as a marble to slightly larger than a golf ball. They are a dark green color when dried and are frequently full of seeds, which, like *P. somniferum*, are edible. These seeds are sometimes a brick-red color and have a smoky, nutty flavor.

You may also find some dried poppies with medium-sized heads surrounded by a thick ring of immature seed pods that look like a sort of mane. These poppies are known as "hens and chicks," and are very potent indeed. Three of these heads are as strong as ten of the regular ones.

You can be even more sure you've got opium poppies if you see a label indicating the plants were grown in Holland or Turkey.

If the pods have been picked before the portals opened up then the seeds remain inside. You can test this by shaking the pod and listening for the rustling seeds. They're like miniature marimbas and in fact can be used as baby rattles. There's a good chance the seeds are viable, so make sure to save them. They can also be used for cooking and save yourself the five bucks the supermarket charges for a little spice-rack container of them.

❧

It was thought for a long time that the best way to extract opium from poppy pods was through the labor-intensive process of carefully slitting each pod, allowing the juice to exude and harden and then painstakingly collecting it later with a simple scraping tool. This is the way it has been done for thousands of years and is still the way it is done in places all over the world today. But the old way has some problems for the modern world.

Slicing the pods also allows for "diversion" of opium when impoverished peasants keep some of the opium and sell it for themselves. The United States has been adamant that opium-producing countries find ways to stop opium diversion, hoping that limited opium supply will mean less heroin on American soil. Turkey, once a major source of heroin, came under special pressure in the late '60s to do something about poppies in the hands of heroin-makers.

So to satisfy the U.S. government and thwart pilfering in the poppy fields of Turkey, the Turkish government set up elaborate safeguards to ensure that the peasants wouldn't dare slit a poppy pod. First, the number of opium-producing provinces was reduced from 42 out of 67 in 1940 to just seven in 1970. In 1971 all poppy cultivation was banned while the government constructed an enormous state-of-the-art alkaloid processing plant in Bolvadin to extract the opium and refine it into various medicines.

Poppies were back again in 1974 and now the government even encouraged poppy production through price supports. To cut down on "pilfering," peasants are made to let the poppy heads dry in the field, harvesting by snapping the whole heads off the plant. To make extra sure there was no hanky-panky, armed guards supervised the work. The peasants are allowed to cut each head horizontally and shake out the seeds, then they must bring the empty heads to the factory. High, but not exorbitant prices are paid. At times the Turkish government has had surplus poppies more than ten years old. This gives an idea of how long dried poppies can keep.

Once the international quota has been reached, some of the surplus poppies are sold off and distributed as floral decorations around the world. You don't have to go to a Laotian opium den to get opium—it's available at K-Mart. Removing it is easy. Becoming your own opium farmer is easy, too!

MAKING POPPY TEA

POPPY HEAD TEA HAS BEEN A FAVORITE IN EUROPE FOR MANY HUNDREDS of years and is still a typical home remedy today. In recent years, poppy tea has been made illegal in various European states, and in America, the legality of tea brewed remains vague.

The first step is to remove about ten heads, and only three heads if you're brewing from the large "gigantheum" variety, and set them aside. This should be enough for one person. By weight it comes out to approximately ten grams, so if you've got a good enough scale and aren't sure how much is enough you can measure it that way.

❖

The next step is to snap off the remainder of the stem from the bottom of the poppy head in such a way as to create a hole there. With a little practice you'll see all it takes is a slight twist as you break off the stem stump. You do this only if there are seeds inside the head (listen for them rattling when you shake the head). Poppy seeds can be put to far better uses than making tea. Hint: be a Johnny Poppyseed and beautify the countryside.

Now simply pour the seeds out of the pod into a bowl. It's not uncommon for a single poppy head to contain a thousand seeds or more. You should be able to collect enough seeds from a single bunch of poppies to ensure poppy crops for the rest of your life.

There are different kinds of seeds. There are the black (or grey) ones you know from poppy seed cake and there are dull red ones. You may also find smaller, lighter colored seeds in shades of brown or tan. These are seeds that failed to mature, probably because the pod wasn't old enough when it was harvested. Keep them, too.

Now take your empty pods and break them with your thumb and fingers as you drop them into a coffee or spice grinder. It is important to use the best grinder you can find; the pods should be ground as finely as possible to expose maximum surface area. Grinding to a powder is ideal. For purposes of making tea, the opium is water-soluble but much harder to get out of bigger chunks of dried poppy. A blender on its highest setting is also good enough. In fact, one way to make tea is to pour boiling water into the blender with the crushed pods and let it blend for a minute or two before straining.

It may sound like obvious advice, but experience has taught me there's no harm in reminding yourself to keep a firm grip on the blender's lid anytime there's liquid inside it. Keep an even tighter grip if that liquid is boiling hot! And use an oven mitt or dish towel over the lid to protect your hand from being scalded.

You can do it that way (using about two cups of water) or you can add the poppy powder to two cups of boiling water in a pot. Immediately remove the pot from the heat and stir the poppies into the brew. An egg-beater is an ideal tool for this. As with the blender, swirl the stuff around for a minute or so.

It's important that you not boil the poppy pods too much. Although it doesn't matter if the water boils for a few seconds, it's not a good idea to let it go on for too long as the heat will begin to break down the opium.

❖

Probably the best way to make poppy tea is with a French press. It allows for plenty of steeping so the tea is nice and strong and the screen keeps the bits of dried poppy out of your mouth when you drink it. Cleanup is a lot easier, too.

However you choose to brew your tea, let it steep for at least ten or 15 minutes. By then the majority of the opium alkaloids have been extracted into the water, but it can't hurt to let it sit for a few minutes while it cools. Some people swear by a long steep, but I'm not sure how much stronger it is. If you like lemon juice in your tea, it's probably not a bad idea to put that in while the tea is steeping as the acids in the juice will help release the alkaloids. Even if you don't like lemon, you might consider adding it for just this reason. Vinegar would do about the same thing, as would vitamin C (ascorbic acid).

Just make sure not to let the tea cook for a long time and risk destroying the alkaloids. Let it cool.

❖

Next, if you've made the tea in a blender or in a pot you've got to pour it through a wire mesh strainer. The kind sold in most grocery stores should work well. The mesh shouldn't be so big that it lets the poppy mash get through nor so fine that it gets clogged up. Some glop showing up at the bottom of your mug is to be expected and, since it contains opium, you may as well swallow it, too.

If you've poured it through the strainer, make sure you mash it down with the bottom of a tumbler or a large spoon to squeeze out all the liquid. The mash can be used again with varying degrees of success and is good for at least one more time (tea drinkers call this "second pass"). To make the most of your poppies, it's a good idea to make to the seed sample caused by preparation procedures required by the tests themselves?

Police fascination with catching drug users when there is no evidence has led to some in-depth studies of poppy seeds that haven't done them much good, but which lopsidedly enrich this nook of poppy science. The problem vexing police has been the morphine and other alkaloids from poppy seeds (which are unassailably legal) ruining fancy piss-tests with what they call "false positives." It doesn't take more than a slice of poppy seed cake or a single bagel to set off the drug abuser alarms on most tests.

So far, the only organization to back down from using pee-tests as serious indicators of opiate use has been the U.S. military. Using pee tests in the way suggested by its manufacturer only results in the costly "weeding out" of law-abiding, drug-free soldiers who can carry out their killing functions perfectly well.

Instead of spending hundreds of millions more for backup tests to further scrutinize urine samples, the military simply increased the threshold level of morphine in urine to a figure ten times higher than used by most employers in the United States. The tests don't measure whether a person is under the influence of a drug or whether he's impaired. They just measure what's in the urine. The Department of Transportation has discovered that nearly 70% of its positive urine tests for opiates are caused by poppy seeds.

According to *Forensic Sci Int* 27: 111–117 (1985), several different lots of seeds from various sources were assayed for morphine and found to range from 4–200 mg/kg.

The original edition of this book cited only one range of figures: 7–60 micrograms of morphine per gram of seeds. It seems the high end of 200 micrograms is much closer to the real upper range of morphine in poppy seeds.

another batch as soon as the first one is finished. For the second cooking, just use half as much water and the wet grounds. This tea will be weaker but still effective.

❖

Be sure to save your stems. They can be ground up and made into tea that's just as potent, though you will have to use two or three times as much powdered stem as head for the same amount of tea.

If your poppies have still have their leaves, save them, too. Strip any leaves off the stems by running them through your fingers, and save them for smoking. It's also possible to smoke the ground-up heads or stems but it's probably not the best use of the plant. The leaves, however, can be broken up and smoked either in a joint or from a pipe. Poppy smoke is thick and acrid, so you may want to run it through a water pipe. The effects are much quicker than the tea but not as long-lasting.

The roots of the poppy contain opium, too, but not all that much and roots don't normally come in bunches from the florist, anyway. If you grow plants and want to do anything with the roots, make sure to give them plenty of time to dry. The thick, fibrous roots are very difficult to cut when fresh.

If you are using fresh poppies (often on sale as cut flowers in florists) you'll find it's not necessary to use boiling hot water and the resulting mixture will be bright green. You can even use cold water to extract fresh poppies, but hot water dissolves more opium alkaloids than cool. Fresh poppies are more potent than dried and you need only half or two-thirds the number of heads to get the same effect.

MAKING OPIUM FROM POPPY TEA

Once you've made opium tea, it's a cinch to make something close to plain old opium by letting the water evaporate off. You can do this

As recently as 1996 forensic scientists at the Armed Forces Institute of Pathology in Washington, D.C. ran GC/MS tests on poppy seeds from India and the Netherlands. They found concentrations of codeine, morphine, thebaine, papaverine, and narcotine (a.k.a. noscapine) were 44, 167, 41, 67, and 230 micrograms/g in Indian poppy seeds, and were 1.8, 39, 1.0, 0.17, 0.84 micrograms/g in Netherlands poppy seeds, respectively.

Then they fed these seeds to some humans, waited a while and tested their urine to find the lowest detectable concentrations of codeine, morphine, thebaine, and papaverine, which turned out to be 4, 4, 5, 0.4, and 4 ng/ml, respectively.

The Indian seeds were found to contain 167 micrograms per gram of seeds; this works out to 167 milligrams of morphine per kilogram (about 2.2 lbs). That sounds low, and it is, except that it also works out to 167 milligrams of morphine per kilo, or a little better than five-and-a-half 30 mg. dollops of dope. Not bad for what can be purchased at the grocery store for eight or ten bucks.

These cops ventured that the detection of narcotine, papaverine, or thebaine in someone's piss could be used to differentiate poppy seed consumption from illicit drug users. There's an obvious and easy way to defeat this: just eat some poppy seeds with your illicit opiates and they will automatically render your pee legal. ✤

best in a glass brownie or casserole dish, letting a small fan play over the surface to speed the process. Alternatively, a crockpot-type slow cooker can be used—just make sure the temperature of the liquid doesn't exceed 70 degrees centigrade (158 degrees Fahrenheit). A day or so later you'll be left with a watery sludge that you'll need to marshal to one corner and continue drying. In this way you'll be able to collect the extract, which is quite sticky.

After it dries a little more you can roll the opium into pea-sized balls and pretend you're in Victorian England or fashion it into festive shapes. Encase the pills in gold leaf and pretend you are a Turkish sultan. You can also use this ersatz opium to make your own laudanum or any of a bunch of concoctions described below. You can also smoke it. This is opium as it has been handled for centuries. A hundred years ago opium traders separated opium into two qualities. Good-quality opium contained 10% morphine, while low-quality contained less. This lesser-quality opium was normally sold as "smoking opium."

The quality of tea opium also depends on the amount of plant material in it. Too much poppy head residue and the opium will be light brown, dry, and flaky. To avoid flaky opium, filter the tea more thoroughly before evaporating. Coffee filters, silk, or muslin cloth can be used. Ideally, the opium should be dark, dark brown and very sticky. It has a somewhat bitter, licorice-like taste and can either be chewed before swallowing or even dissolved under the tongue. Some people really hate the taste, however.

While the product you get from evaporating poppy tea made from opium poppies is not, strictly speaking, the same as opium, it is close enough to use as raw material for producing your own morphine and heroin.

OTHER WAYS OF TAKING OPIUM

Laudanum

EARLY RECIPES FOR LAUDANUM CALL FOR ALL KINDS OF THINGS IN THE mixture but today, laudanum is made mainly from grain alcohol and water. The easiest way to make it is to dissolve as much opium as possible into pure grain alcohol, then dilute it to about 50 proof. The laudanum can be flavored in any way you like, using spices or even sugar. It's also possible to dissolve opium into hard liquors like whisky or tequila for a modern take on laudanum. The alcohol preserves the opium and also speeds its delivery into the bloodstream.

Other opium preparations have similar origins to laudanum, meaning there have been many recipes over time. Among these preparations are Paregoric (opium mixed with camphor) and Black Drop (opium with ipecac). Black Drop-type opium preparations use water and not alcohol. Pulverized opium was once mixed into an ointment for topical use. There are literally hundreds of different recipes calling for opium and the stuff has been mixed with such dubious ingredients as chloroform, soap, ox-gall, and lead. Don't forget the frog sperm.

A successful Laudanum recipe by "Fogle" is printed at the end of this chapter.

Smoking Opium

SMOKING AS A WAY OF INGESTING OPIUM HAS BEEN PRACTICED SINCE ANCIENT Greece. But in modern times, opium smoking was popularized, if not invented, by the Chinese and has since become something of an art form. The exotic ritualism of opium smoking can be seen in Errol Flynn's description of smoking opium with his Chinese girlfriend.

Opium prepared for smoking is called a "hop" (we get our expressions "hopped-up" and "hop-head" from this) and is normally made from opium of less than ten percent morphine content. This kind of opium is normally rejected by opium buyers who need to guarantee a certain potency to their customers.

Before smoking, the opium must be prepared by someone who is skilled in the art of making the "pill," known as "chefing" in America. The "chef" uses a pair of needles called *yen-hok* to manipulate the opium over a flame, drying and heating it at the same time. When the pill (or *yen-pok*) is ready, it is quickly inserted into the bowl of an opium pipe and heated further. Opium is not burned but heated, which creates vapor rather than smoke. The vapor carries the alkaloids straight to the bloodstream via the lungs.

The residue left in an opium pipe is called *yen-shee* and contains a lot of morphine. Hopheads can either smoke this residue again or mix it into their coffee. It is treated somewhat like the dregs of a beer barrel and typically, yen-shee is left over for poor folks who can't afford proper opium.

If the opium is any good, it takes no more than a couple of lungfuls to knock the smoker back onto his back, usually with his head in a pillow. There he lies, taking tokes off his pipe as needed for hours or days. Often, a constantly burning alcohol lamp is kept nearby so the opium smoker need only swing his or her pipe over the flame to resume smoking.

Yen-shee is scraped away with a tool called a *yen-shee gow*. Skilled opium chefs used to be prized by opium smokers who often gave the chef money in addition to letting him or her smoke for free.

Another way to smoke opium is by "chasing the dragon"—placing the opium on a piece of tin foil and heating it from below. When the smoke begins to rise, the smoker sucks it up through a short straw. This is a good way to smoke fresh opium that hasn't had a chance to dry yet.

Injection, Snorting, Etc.

Opium can be injected and it has been done but it is not a good way to take opium. Usually injections of opium (and wine) have been done only as experiments on dogs... and a lot of the dogs died. Since opium is a fairly solid substance, it's hard to inject without diluting and is hard to dilute in the first place. Also, opium may easily contain plant fibers or other contaminants that can cause serious and even lethal infections. Don't shoot opium.

Yes, you can snort opium. Dissolve it into some hot water and suck it up your nose. This is not a popular method today, but I'd bet it was done, like everything else, in Ancient Greece.

To maximize the effects of opium, take it on an empty or nearly empty stomach. This gives it a better crack at your bloodstream.

The amino acid tyrosine might either potentiate or extend the effects of opium. Tyrosine is one of the major building blocks of endorphins and it's possible that extra tyrosine will prevent the breakdown of opium you take into your system.

Don't forget to try poppy salad. The larger leaves are as crunchy and tasty as romaine, with the bonus of built-in opium dressing. Some people also like to chop up the heads and sprinkle them onto their salads. The stems are a little too fibrous to eat.

Both leaves and stems can also be smoked. The effect is a sort of an "instant nod" that dissipates within ten minutes. Poppy smoke is harsh, so it's best to smoke it through a water pipe.

Opiate absorption is inhibited by taking antacids, so lay off the Tums while eating opium. At the same time you might try mixing some lime or lemon juice into your poppy tea as it's brewing—theoretically the acetic acid (which is present in the juice as part of the larger corboxylic acid, citric acid) should transform a very small amount of the morphine into heroin over time. Apple cider vinegar, which contains around 4%

acetic acid, should have the same effect.

Please note that the above suggestion is theory only and would be a terrible way to make heroin. It's just a way to add a little bang to your opium. Other ways might mix aspirin and/or acetaminophen into your opium, as it's been shown to slowly convert at least some of the morphine there into heroin.

FOGLE'S GUIDE TO MAKING (A SORT OF) LAUDANUM

We reproduce here a helpful fellow from the Netherlands' recipe on making a form of laudanum, the popular nineteenth-century opium and alcohol drink. See http://forum.poppies.org/index.php?showtopic=10790 for images.

Real Laudanum was made with opium and many other ingredients. Among which were henbane, nutmeg and lots of others. My type of Laudanum is actually an alcoholic extract of concentrated poppy tea. That is why I wouldn't label my bottles Laudanum but the made-up name: Laudrum. There are numerous ways to make such a concoction. I don't claim mine is the best or even any good. But the result of the following is a nice-tasting liqueur with a good opiate buzz. And the best thing: no chemicals or fancy equipment needed.

To make two liters of Laudrum you need:

Ingredients

1) dried poppies (ca. 2.3 kg with seeds = 1.0 kg without the seeds)
2) alcohol (1 liter 80%)
3) aniseed, star anise and/or fennel
4) sugar and dextrose (glucose)
5) water

Materials

1) several big pans
2) filter cloth (old T-shirt)
3) several plastic buckets
4) several glass jars
5) stove
6) water bath
7) some cutlery, spatula etc.
8) 50 ml syringe or turkey baster (optional)

Poppies

This is my recipe and I don't buy poppies. I grow poppies. So get some seeds, find a deserted plot somewhere in suburbia, and spread them. You can either harvest them and dry them at home, or let them dry in the field. They will be dry about one month after they bloomed. But beware: heavy rainfall will flush all goodies from your pods.

Crush dried poppies. Separate the seeds from the straw by using a kitchen sieve. Use the seeds for food or next year's harvest. You can use a blender to make the straw even finer. But you don't want it to be too powdery at this stage, or it will make it harder to filter in a later step.

Alcohol

Americans can use Everclear. I use 80% Stroh Rum. The rum is mixed with activated charcoal, from the fish-pond store, and left for a week or so. The rum should be clear and colorless after this, with no smell other than that of alcohol. This I call "reclaimed rum."

Let's get started.

Step 1

Get a pan that holds your poppies, maybe 10 liters. Or several pans. Put your poppy straw (1 kg) in the pan(s) and cover with water (about 7 liters). Bring to a boil and let simmer for 30 minutes max.

Step 2

Pull the filter cloth over a bucket and secure with a string. Carefully pour the water from the pan into the bucket. Leave as much poppies in the pan as possible. You will get 3 liters of water in the bucket.

Step 3

Add as much fresh water to the pan as you strained off. In this case it is 3 liters. Bring to a simmer and leave for another 30 min. Strain again.

Step 4

Repeat step 3. Now we have done three extractions which gave us about 8 liters of extract. And brown mushy poppies. Throw away the poppies.

Step 5

This is going to be tricky. The problem is this: we have a lot of water to evaporate. Water boils at a temperature at which morphine becomes instable. What chemical reaction takes place at these temps is a mystery to me, but it is no good. A temperature of 85°C seems to be a safe upper limit. But at 85°C water takes ages to evaporate. Tests have shown that morphine doesn't rot away immediately at 100°C, it takes time. So we can boil this water off as long as we do it fast! My solution is to do relatively small portions at a time. With a fan blowing dry air over the boiling pots, effectively cooling the solution to almost sub-boiling temps by evaporation of water. This way no part of the extract is exposed to boiling temps for more than 15 minutes or so. Use large shallow pans, maybe the lids of pans. Don't let the extract get too thick. If it gets too thick, there is very little water left, so it can easily get too hot, ruining your alkaloids. You have got to stop boiling while you can still pour the extract as a liquid. For reference: you should have about 1 to 2 liters left.

I am sure there must be much better ways to get water out of an extract. But this one is simple, only requires kitchen stuff, and a day of work. Maybe the handier types of folk would construct a vacuum rotation film evaporator that can evaporate at lower temp and with greater speed.

Step 6

Set up a water bath, preferably with a thermostat, and evaporate most of the last water. With a fan over the liquid it should take about 12 hours to reduce the last one liter to about 500 mls. You can use a boiling water bath, because the evaporating water will cool your solution down (fan!). Make sure your bath does not boil dry! If you have a thermostat bath, set it to 85 °C. How dry? You don't want a dry crust; we want something we can scoop like thick maple syrup.

Step 7

Fill jars half with the thick gooey extract and fill up with 80% alcohol. Shake a few minutes. Leave for a day and shake again. Now leave for a week or longer.

Step 8

In time the alcohol and extract will have separated again, with a dark brown clear upper layer and a lighter murky bottom layer. Now we want the upper portion without any bottom silt. This can be done by decanting, or better, use a big syringe. Keep the clear upper layer in a large bottle.

Step 9

Refill the jar, still half full with sediment, now with 40% (or 50%) alcohol. Shake, wait a day, shake, wait a week and separate like in step 8.

Step 10

This is the same as step 9 but now with 20% alcohol. After siphoning off the last top layer, you can throw away the slurry. It should be depleted. The reason I go down on the percentage of alcohol is an economic one. This way the loss of alcohol in the final sediment layer is minimal.

Step 11

Mix the 80%, 40% and 20% extracts together. Now we have about 1.5 liters of dark brown liquid, which should contain the best part of 1 liter of 80% alcohol. All we have to do is add some flavor and dilute it in the end to 2 litres of 40% papaver liqueur.

Step 12

This is the best part: the flavoring. This is where we can make a difference. Like the difference between moonshine and a 10-year-old single malt. Both do the job but they don't taste the same, right?

My personal favorite recipe is (for two liters):

> 20 grams of aniseed
> 5 grams of star anise
> 15 grams of fennel seed
> 200 grams of sugar
> 350 grams of dextrose/glucose

Other good active ingredients are Ginkgo Biloba or Ma Huang. Both have a good synergy with the laudanum and they add nice taste too. Another variation is to replace the "reclaimed rum" with Ouzo, Pernod or Pastis. You will need three bottles of 70cl though. But you spare yourself the trouble of reclaiming rum. And no need to make the final product to taste: the ouzo and raw laudanum taste good enough.

Just a quick recap:

1) Simmer grinded poppy straw in water for a maximum of 30 minutes
2) Filter
3) Do step 1 and 2 a second time
4) Do step 1 and 2 a third time and combine filtrates
5) Boil of excess water quickly in small batches with a fan blowing over the surface
6) Evaporate the last bit of water with a water bath; direct heat would get too hot
7) Fill a jar halfway with the extract, add alcohol, shake, wait a bit, shake, wait a week
8) Siphon off the top layer = raw laudanum/laudrum
9) Add fresh alcohol, shake, wait a bit, shake, wait a week for the second time and separate like in step 8
10) Add fresh alcohol, shake, wait a bit, shake, wait a week for the third time and separate like in step 8
11) Mix all the alcohol extracts together and dilute to about 40%
12) Bring to taste, make a nice label and you are READY!

Yours,
Fogle

CHAPTER 4
POPPY CULTIVATION

CHAPTER 4 ❖ POPPY CULTIVATION

THE BEST WAY TO ENSURE A GOOD SUPPLY OF OPIUM IS TO grow your own opium poppies. With fresh poppies you have the opportunity to harvest pure, fresh opium directly from the pod. You can even coax opium poppies into producing more opium than otherwise by "milking" them—incising a head twice or more over time.

And you still have heads and straw for making tea.

A lot of what is known about poppy cultivation comes to us from British documents of the eighteenth century back when the Empire was growing so much of it for export to China. Research into poppy cultivation essentially came to an end soon after the twentieth century began and didn't pick up again until the 1970s when drug companies set up operations in Tasmania and devoted intense study to everything to do with opium poppies.

The only poppies that produce latex with appreciable amounts of morphine are the *Papaver somniferum* and a wild poppy called *Papaver setigerum*. Seeds for this second kind of plant are available but its opium is weaker and it is not extensively cultivated. Still, if you get hold of some seeds, it would be fun to grow some, especially if you would crossbreed them with *somniferum* to produce an opium-producing hybrid. The California poppy (*Eschscholzia californica*) isn't a true poppy at all and does not have opium in it.

The poppy's alkaloid-containing latex is produced in different parts of the plant and is present throughout the poppy plant, including the leaves. But opium is most concentrated in the seed capsule. As the poppy matures and the seed capsule grows larger and ripens, more and more opium is to be found there. Although the majority of opium is collected by slicing the capsules and gathering the opium that runs out, it is possible to extract opium from any part of the plant, even the seeds.

Poppy seeds contain morphine in amounts varying from 7 micrograms to 200 micrograms per gram. The seeds contain codeine, too. This is a low-potency source for opium but it is strong enough to be used medicinally in small animals and it's why the urine of people who eat poppy seeds tests positive for opiates.

It's theoretically possible to extract opium from poppy seed bought at your local grocery store. Even if the seeds are old or have been sterilized the morphine remains. In fact, other items available at the grocery store make it possible to not only extract morphine but to purify and strengthen it.

The strength and amount of the opium produced by your poppies depends mostly on genetics. Sunlight and soil composition are also important factors but not decisive in and of themselves, Other factors such as altitude and wind figure into the makeup of a plant's opium.

The main thing is to make sure the plants have enough nutrients in the form of fertilizer and plenty of sunlight. Poppies, like other plants, tend to deplete the soil so it's good to practice crop rotation or use fertilizer if you want to grow them year after year. Any kind of manure is a good fertilizer but some of the best organic fertilizers are different types of bird manure. It is of the right pH, and contains phosphorus, which poppies need.

❖

The exact role of opium for the poppy plant is not understood. All plants have juice or sap that carries nutrients around the plant, but why this particular poppy should produce opium is a matter of speculation.

Some think opium is so useful, so uncannily like chemicals needed by the brain, that the poppy is a divine gift to mankind. Maybe so, but if evolutionary science has any truth to it then the sap should be of benefit to the poppy, too. There must be a reason the poppy contains opium and not some other sap. How is this substance of advantage to the plant?

Opium could serve as a deterrent to predators. The alkaloids in the opium (like morphine) are bitter-tasting and poisonous to small animals. Any animal looking for sugar would quickly deem the poppy a bad choice. At the same time the alkaloids are potent enough to serve as an effective insect repellent if not insecticide. Poppies are very resistant to bugs and it's only after they have matured and sent their seeds on their way that the opium begins to dry and aphids (their chief insect foe) or other insects begin to feed on them.

It is also curious that those plants that are attacked by insects seem to be singled out, leaving the rest alone. Perhaps you'll find that only one head in a patch containing 50 or more heads will succumb to insects. In this case, don't collect seeds from that head.

Birds, too, love poppy seeds but don't normally try to eat them while they're still in the pod. Those that do have long thin beaks, which pierce the opium-filled wall surrounding the seed chambers, and are not affected by the opium.

Some say the color of a poppy's bloom reveals the presence or strength of the flower's opium. It does not but the legend persists. Even DEA agents looking for poppies have been quoted in the mainstream press as scouting out the "characteristic red opium poppy." Lots of opium poppies are red but they can also be white, blue, pink, purple or shades in between. The color of the petals makes no difference in the opium. Opium poppies are sometimes described in old herbals as "White Poppies."

Poppies can grow in almost any soil and even do well in slightly sandy or rocky places. Generally, poppies do well in loose, loamy soil and don't grow easily in clay or other dense soils. But any soil can be modified to accommodate poppies. It has been said that poppies are like weeds because they grow so easily. That's not exactly true, but poppies tend to thrive even in bad conditions and poppies grow in almost any climate.

It is often asserted that poppies require very specific climates to thrive, and even knowledgeable botanists have flatly declared that the opium poppy is a tropical plant and will not grow where it gets cold.

OPIUM POPPIES GROWN AT THE SIDE OF AN APARTMENT BUILDING IN SEATTLE.

And an article in *Details* magazine asserted that poppies require an elevation of at least 3,000 feet. Neither of those claims are true.

Some of the confusion about where poppies will grow may have to do with the temperatures poppies like. Poppies do best where it is cool. The seedlings, especially, thrive in temperatures in the high 40s and the seeds sprout when it's only a few degrees above freezing. In tropical areas, where the sun is always strong, poppies are normally grown high in the mountains where it stays cool. This is probably why poppies do so well along the coast in the Pacific Northwest where the elevation is low, but the temperatures are cool despite long days in the spring and summer.

OPIUM POPPIES RUNNING RAMPANT ON WASHINGTON STATE GOVERNMENT LAND.

STILL, POPPIES GROW ANYWHERE.

POPPIES HAVE BEEN PRODUCED ALL OVER THE UNITED STATES. OPIUM crops have been a source of revenue for early American farmers in Pennsylvania, Vermont, New Hampshire and Massachusetts. By the 1870s, farms in Florida, Louisiana, California, and Arizona were reporting yields as high as 120 pounds of opium per acre. During the Civil War, the South got opium from farms in Virginia, Tennessee, South Carolina, and Georgia.

It should be noted that all this opium cultivation was taking place during a time when the annual per capita consumption of imported opium was already 52 grains (330 mgs) per person—enough to supply everybody with a hefty weekly dose. Apparently there was more demand than could be met by the fields of India and China, and America was on the verge of becoming an opium-producing nation itself.

The cultivation of opium poppies was banned in 1942, but the opium poppy has already established itself very firmly all over the country. Opium poppies grow wild in urban Seattle. They grow wild in frigid, windswept Iowa. Poppies are everywhere! And poppies grown for ornamental purposes are legal... but might cause you trouble anyway.

In areas of the Pacific Northwest, DEA agents are known to cruise older neighborhoods looking for the flowers and then asking the owners to destroy them. In 1992, a DEA man vacationing in Idaho made a pest of himself in one small town by tromping into at least two people's gardens and ripping up all the poppies he saw there.

When the shocked residents noticed a man destroying their gardens, they called the police who came to investigate. The DEA agent's antics did not endear him or the federal government to either the local cops or the town's residents.

In the years since then, federal drug authorities have seriously increased their response to people caught growing or selling poppies, sending more than one person to prison. But these prosecutions don't seem to be part of any overarching policy. There hasn't been any crackdown on companies selling poppy seeds, the use or sale of dried ornamental poppies, or on poppies grown in people's gardens. It's not easy to say where they draw the line.

Still, poppies are grown for ornamental purposes in gardens in many older sections of American cities have proven to be good sources of poppies.

Poppy crops are also most certainly being grown in a number of states, some of them perhaps under the auspices of the U.S. government (probably in southern Oregon), which has at times experimented with domestic production of opium. California, too, has been the source of acres of fresh-cut poppies for sale all along the West Coast.

❖

The plant itself sends up one main stem, which branches into several, thinner stems sort of like a candelabra. It is at the end of each of these stems that the plant forms a bulb, which is normally pointed downward as if the flower were hanging its head. To multiply the number of heads per plant, pinch off the first bud that forms. This causes the plant to produce a number of new shoots, each with a seed head. A poppy plant normally produces between three and five heads. The leaves of the poppy are a kind of dusty "glaucous" green, and the edges are softly serrated. From a distance, young poppy plants look a lot like dandelions.

As each bulb or pod matures, it splits and rises up, eventually spreading out into the flower with a small seed head in the middle. At this time the head may be no bigger than the eraser on the end of a pencil but it will have the distinctive crown.

The flowers typically don't last too long, a couple of weeks at most, before the petals fall off. Some poppies bloom for only a few days before they start dropping their petals. Although the petals aren't too fragrant, it's still possible to make perfume from them, and in the old days, they were used to wrap balls of opium—looking like red paper and even tinting the opium a bit.

Now the head begins to grow in earnest. Some say they are "ripe" ten days after the petals fall off, but this is not a hard and fast rule and ripeness can take as long as three weeks. Inside, the head is divided into eight to 12 vertical, crescent-shaped seed chambers. At first these seeds are soft, white beads that gradually ripen inside the head. This ripening can even occur inside poppy heads that have been severed from the plant and refrigerated. As the seeds ripen and dry, the head grows.

At this stage the poppy doesn't need any more water and the opium it produces will be more concentrated and potent if the plant stays dry. In fact, heavy rains during this time can leach the alkaloids out of the plant and weaken the opium. Poppies are also susceptible to rot should the ground become waterlogged. For this reason, it's best to plant poppies on a 20- to 40-degree slope for good drainage.

Once the head reaches maximum size, tiny portals to the seed chambers open up just beneath the crown and the wind begins to draw the dried poppy seeds from inside. Outside the capsule, the seeds are either carried by the wind or upon water or even carried away by ants.

Poppy seeds—red or black—are very small, and look like tiny specks to the naked eye. But take a magnifying glass to them and you'll see the seeds are kidney-shaped, slightly elongated and pitted with regular indentations forming a pattern over the skin of the seed. Under stronger magnification (50X) the skin of the seed looks like a peanut's.

HOW TO PLANT

PLANTING IS DONE BY THROWING OR BROADCASTING—THAT MEANS YOU just toss them out over moist soil and let them fall where they may. The seeds are so small they just disappear into the dirt; even those left on top of the soil will sprout. Some suggest covering the seeds with a light coat of soil after planting and this would be a good idea if you live in a cold climate, as the coating of soil will provide insulation against early frost. For planting large areas, use one of those grass seed broadcasting gizmos designed to plant lawns.

To ensure that the seeds drop into the dirt, and to give the plants room to grow, the soil should be plowed. With deeply plowed soil, it's possible to sow poppies two or three times in a row for a single crop, as was the old practice in India. This method produces maximum production per square foot, but planting must be done carefully and evenly to avoid "thick spots" where the poppy sprouts seem to cause the ground to erupt with poppy shoots, which then strangle each other out. Mix the seed with sand—about one part seed to three parts sand mix is good. This is a good idea anyway since poppy seeds are so small, it's hard to throw them evenly.

One rule of thumb is to use one pound of poppy seeds per acre of land.

The flower likes slightly acidic soil, which you don't have to prepare much. It's not strictly necessary to plow or turn the soil before planting, and poppies will even grow well in soil that already has grass growing in it.

It's not necessary and not even advisable to sprout the seeds in between wet paper towels as with some plants. Poppy seedlings have very fragile, hair-like roots and you're sure to ruin them if you try to handle them. Plant them where you want to grow them and then thin them out once they are a few weeks old.

The soil should be thoroughly watered and allowed to dry a bit before planting. After planting, keep the soil moist, but not wet. If the ground is too wet the young plants are prone to attack by fungus or rot. Bacterial blight, too, can happen and plants that show signs of this should be culled, although applications of fungicide have been shown to be helpful.

The seeds sprout within a week or two. Misting or sprinkling the sprouts is a fine way to water them and you should give them a little every day sort of like a heavy dew. Once the flower appears, however, you should stop watering the plant altogether.

❖

Poppies are ancient plants and, although delicate at first, are pretty hardy. You should find that most seeds that you plant will sprout. You may need to thin them out so that each plant has a few inches room between it and the next one. Experts argue about distance between plants: either six inches to two feet. The bigger they grow, the more space they'll need. Plants growing only two or three feet tall can do with just six inches of spacing. Monster plants over six feet tall need much more. Since most plants in North America grow to a height of only three to five feet, a foot between plants should be about right.

When planting a large area, it's less important that the poppies have room than to allow some space for a human to get in to tend the plants.

You can plant poppies both in fall and the spring. If planted when it's cold outside, you may find they don't sprout right away and that's fine. If they do sprout some of the plants may be killed by the winter's cold, but

Cultivated poppy field in Tasmania.

not all. Even poppies that seem dead from a frost have a chance of coming back once it warms up. Opium poppies have been successfully sown in England as late as December.

The plants grow slowly or stop growth during the cold and begin to grow at the end of winter where the combination of cold, moist ground and lengthening days is perfect for them. If you haven't planted in the fall, then do so as early in the spring as possible. It's been said that the best place to plant poppies is at the edge of melting snow, so this should give you an idea of both soil temperature and moisture level poppies like.

Poppies do have enemies besides rot. One danger comes just after planting when birds arrive to feast on the nutritious seeds. Still, even with birds eating them, there always seem to be enough seeds that escape and you'll still have a crop.

As seedlings, poppies are also favorites of cutworms, which can be thwarted by placing a metal collar around the plant (you can make these out of soft drink cans). Just sink the collar about an inch into the ground and leave about that much above it, and that should be adequate.

Rabbits, too, love the succulent little poppies, so try to keep the critters away from the plants until they sprout their secondary leaves.

High winds or hard rains can tear up poppies, so if possible, keep them protected by planting them near some sort of windbreak. Right up next to the house is one idea. Another method, used in Southeast Asia, is to plant poppies on ground where corn has already been harvested and the stalks left standing. The stalks act as protectors for the small plants without blocking the sun.

After the plant gets a running start there's not much for you to do. Of course, keeping them watered and fortifying the soil can only help, and the popp will produce better and more opium if you use a little fertilizer and make sure they get enough sun. You can also mix the crop with rhubarb, potatoes, turnips, or whatever else will make room for the poppy plant. Other than that you can ignore them.

Indoor poppies can be planted in potting soil just as you would outside. Just remember to plant them in the container you mean for them to stay in (or else use peat cups) as transplanting poppies is never easy.

Happily, the poppy does not have very deep roots at all and a five-foot plant with 20 heads and a stem three-quarters of an inch thick may have a root only a few inches deep. Plus, a poppy's root tends to grow downward for a bit, then grow horizontally, making it even easier to grow in shallow soil. Pots eight or ten inches deep are probably sufficient, but bigger is better.

❖

Lighting for your poppies is the same as for any other plant. Any sort of grow light will serve—even cheap, incandescent bulbs. Bluish light seems to be best for normal growth, while reds bring on flowering. The greatest difficulty posed by indoor poppy-growing is the problem of too much heat. Remember, poppies like cool temperatures and lots of light, a combination that's hard to get with incandescent bulbs. The best lighting for poppies would be from an array of some of the latest LED lighting arrays that have only recently come close to being a feasible answer to the problem of getting lots of light without much heat. Fluorescent lights are another possibility, as is using the more typical metal halide lamp setups along with some kind of air-conditioning or even refrigeration. Of course, in that last case, your electric bill is going to be quite a bit higher than normal.

The most important thing about lighting for poppies is that it approximate its growing season. Poppies bloom in the summer, so try to start out with a shorter day (say 14 hours or so) and gradually add to that as time goes on. For flowering, keep the lights on up to 18 hours a day. But remember to keep the temperature down. Fluorescent or halide lights along with a fan will help a lot.

Until there is a lot more research done into the indoor growing of poppies (like that devoted to orchids or marijuana) it's best to try to mimic nature. But there's nothing wrong with a little experimentation—it's virgin territory.

❖

Most cops aren't looking for poppies and don't know what they look like. And many are only able to recognize certain varieties at certain times, like red poppies in bloom. Because so many people associate opium poppies with red petals (and to a lesser extent white) it's a good idea to plant pink or violet ones. The same reason applies to planting poppies with double leaves. Pink poppies with double petals look just like carnations—little puff balls.

Of course, such unusual flowers might attract attention by themselves, in which case you can just invent a fitting name for them. Many nurseries sell opium poppies under names like "Hungarian Blue Poppies" or some other name.

In any event, the colored petals are only on the plant for a short time. Then they fall off leaving a lower profile but distinctive seed head. These heads are unmistakable to a poppy lover. They can get comments from neighbors.

Poppies can also be interspersed among wildflowers with longer-lasting blooms that get all the attention. They can be hidden by planting them alongside a fence or in a thin row that follows the curves of a creek or property line. Poppies don't have particularly bushy leaves and the whole plant tends to grow upward so from the top they don't present a distinctive profile. It is possible to have hundreds of plants growing in a long line and undetectable from overhead.

Unfortunately you can't hide poppies by planting them beneath trees or any other kind of cover since you'll block too much sun. But working in your favor is the tendency for "spotters" to be scanning the ground for marijuana, not poppies, and their eyes or equipment will be geared toward that. Planting poppies amid other flowers is another way to hide them from the air. An enormous patch of flowers can contain lots of opium poppies.

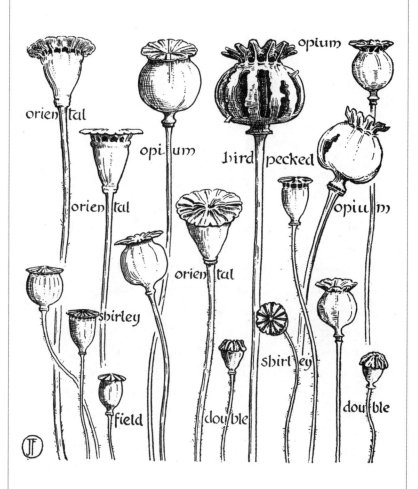

oriental

oriental

shirley

field

opium

opium

oriental

double

opium

bird pecked

shirley

opium

double

WHERE TO GET SEEDS

A GREAT PLACE TO GET SEEDS IS FROM THE FIRST POPPIES YOU BUY IN THE craft store. Failing that, you can buy poppy seeds from the grocery store, where they're for sale as a condiment. There is a potential drawback to grocery-store seeds, though. They may not be viable. They say that store-bought seeds are sterilized, but all the grocery-store seeds have had high rates of sprouting. Sometimes it requires an extra week or so for them to sprout, but they do sprout. Ebay auctions are also full of poppies and seeds.

Grocery-store poppy seeds, bought in the cute little glass bottles in the spice section, are probably from some of the world's best opium cultivars. The seeds are a bit expensive (a bottle costs three or four dollars and contains the same amount of seed you can pour out of a half-dozen good-sized heads), but they probably come from the poppy fields of Tasmania.

Beginning in 1970, two companies—Britain's Glaxo and America's Johnson & Johnson—have invested great energy into transforming the island into the world's most effective poppy country. Tasmania's poppies are said to have some of the highest yields in the world. The seeds from these poppies are a rich blue color and the flower they grow is white.

In some grocery stores, poppy seeds can be found in the bulk food section of the store. These cost just few dollars a pound and always seem to sprout!

Another good place to obtain poppy seeds is from any of a number of mail-order seed companies such as Thompson and Morgan (P.O. Box 1308, Jackson, NJ 08527). Although it costs $1.50 or $2.00 for a pack of a few hundred seeds, they offer some distinct advantages. Besides being guaranteed viable, they can also be selected for color, type of flower and variety. Remember, there are many different forms of opium poppy—these companies even sell the luscious "hens and chickens" strain.

Note: When contacting seed companies, don't talk about opium with them. Same goes in a nursery or a garden supply house (where *Papaver somniferum* can also be found). Some of these people have already gotten a visit from law enforcement officials and might be a little edgy. Some have already withdrawn *Papaver somniferum* seeds from their catalogs.

HARVESTING

HERE'S THE LABOR-INTENSIVE PART OF OPIUM FARMING. IT MAY BE THE reason it never caught on in Europe, where generally child labor was exploited for opium cultivation—child labor that could be so much better exploited at the factories.

There is no hard and fast rule on when to harvest the opium from the ripe capsules. There are a lot of theories about the correct time and method for collecting opium (slice at sunset or dawn, collect at midday, etc.), but there are really many different ways to do it, all of them following the same general rules.

About ten days after the petals fall off, the capsules should have taken on a dusty or frosted appearance and this is one of the signs the opium is ready. Another sign is when the edges of the flower's "crown" begin to turn upward or at least straight out from the head. At this time, the opium may even begin to seep through invisible cuts in the capsule or build up just under the outer skin forming little bruises or spots. This is another sign it's time to harvest.

To get the opium out of the plant, make a very shallow incision longitudinally into the first layer of skin on the poppy head. Normally the knife is drawn from bottom to top in a single, smooth motion. This cut must be very shallow (about one millimeter) for optimum results. Of course, any cut in the pod's skin will quickly bring opium out of the plant.

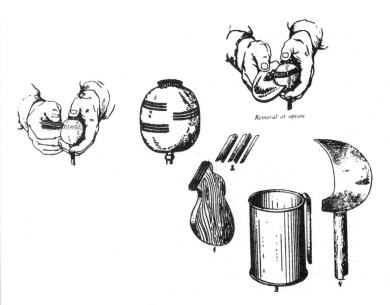

Removal of opium

S<small>CORING THE</small> P<small>OPPY</small> P<small>OD</small>.

It's okay to make horizontal cuts, or cuts at an angle. One popular way to wound a capsule is to cut a sort of V-shape. The important part is to cut only the outer layer of the capsule to get at the milk, without piercing the inner walls and letting some of the opium ooze into the seed pod. Too shallow cuts can cause just enough opium to ooze out to quickly form a crust, sealing the cut and preventing any more opium from coming out. Another old method of harvesting opium is to snip off the heads, gather them together and pierce each one a few times with thick needles. Then the heads are left to ooze all night, and the opium is gathered in the morning.

Old opium hands in Turkey and Iran have many different tools they use to slice the pod and collect the opium, but you can use an Exacto knife, a razor blade, or even a sharp pocket knife. It is possible to make a cutting device with a guide to prevent the blade from going too deep and there are multi-bladed tools for just such a purpose. But a light touch and a sharp blade are sufficient.

As soon as the skin is cut, the opium will bead out along the incision, forming little droplets. As the opium dries, it thickens and turns brown, a fairly quick process. Typically, opium farmers do the slicing in the morning or in the evening and then allow the opium to dry on the pod while the wound heals. After the opium has dried, a dull blade or spoon is used to scrape up the gummy brown opium and save it in a cup or other container until full. The process is repeated until the opium has been collected into kilo-sized balls or cakes.

❖

Another way to collect opium is to place aluminum foil "collars" around the base of the poppy pod to catch any of the opium that drips down the pod toward the stem.

It's not necessary to allow the opium to dry before collection. In fact, this may be easier as the opium is much more fluid before evaporation. The opium as it comes from the plant is also immediately ready to smoke or eat. In fact, you can just lick the opium off the pod right there in the field.

By slicing (wounding) alternate sides of the plant a poppy can be induced to make more opium, thus letting you milk it for two or three harvests before leaving it alone. But the plant may not survive the first wounding. Eventually the slicing will overpower the plant and cut the head to ribbons. The very largest and juiciest pods should be left alone for seed selection and not cut at all so as much energy is put into seed production as possible.

As described in the tea section, opium can also be extracted from the poppy by hot water. Opium is also soluble in alcohol and in ether, but the latter is very explosive, expensive and its mere purchase can put you and a photocopy of your ID on a DEA list. These methods are generally best used with dried poppy plants (also called straw) as is done in Turkey. By far the easiest way to get opium is to collect it in the time-honored way with a sharp knife. This means you get pure opium from the very beginning and don't have to deal with getting rid of solvents.

Opium will keep for a long time, many years if stored correctly. The best way is to seal the opium to protect it from the air and moisture. This keeps the opium from drying out, (although drying won't hurt it and only increases its shelf life) but doesn't permit oxidation or growth of fungi or bacteria. In the old days, poppy petals or "oil-proof" paper were used. After that the wrapped opium should be put into another sealed container, like a cookie tin, and kept in a cool, dry place, away from sunlight. You can freeze opium but that is not necessary.

Storing the opium immersed in alcohol is also possible, but be aware that it will tend to dissolve and make laudanum. Once the alcohol is saturated, though, no more opium will dissolve. ❖

CHAPTER 5
PAPAVER SOMNIFERUM
AND OPIOID DRUGS

Let no one say to me: "Habit forces the smoker to increase the dose." One of the riddles of opium is that the smoker never has to increase his dose.

— Jean Cocteau, *Opium* —

If he takes care of himself, an addict who inhales twelve pipes a day all his life will not only be fortified against influenza, colds and sore throats, but will also be far less in danger than a man who drinks a glass of brandy or who smokes four cigars. I know people who have smoked one, three, seven, up to twelve pipes a day for forty years.

— Jean Cocteau, *Opium* —

FOR ALL THE PASSIONATE TALK ABOUT OPIUM, KNOWLedge about opium is scarce. As a result, our society has become alienated from the realities of the substance. Opium is almost mythical, symbolic of a sort of delicious evil or forbidden happiness.

But even if information about opium and opium poppies weren't so thoroughly suppressed, a full understanding of it eludes even the scientists who have devoted their careers to its study.

The United Nations published a review (in 1994) of its Narcotics Laboratory's 50 years of efforts to identify and describe opium from anywhere in the world. They concluded that despite all the technological advances in the laboratory and the application of computers to the task, they still had a long way to go. Their biggest hurdle was the lack of a larger, more extensive reference collection of opium samples of known origin. For all the inquiry into opium, the stuff remains a mystery.

Opium is the juice or latex produced by the poppy plant known as *Papaver somniferum*. There are lots of varieties of poppy—the Papaveraceae family has six genera and within the genus we find six species. *Somniferum* is the "opium poppy," although other poppies—particularly its close relative *Papaver setigerum*—also contain a goodly amount of morphine. Research at the USDA provides information finding morphine to be present in five species of Papaver (besides *somniferum* and *setigerum*, there is. *P. rhoeas, pseudo-orientale, and orientale*). Other researchers have found morphine in even more poppies (*P. commutatum, P. dubium*) but also in poppies of a different genus. Morphine has been detected in the non-Papaver poppy, the "California Poppy" (*Eschscholzia californica*), in a type of mulberry and even in one of beer's most crucial ingredients, hops.

A SCORED POPPY POD EXUDES ITS LATEX.

Still another poppy, *Papaver bracteatum*, produces quite a bit of the valuable alkaloid thebaine (stopping short of morphine). But it also produces codeine, which is just one enzymatic step away from morphine— and too close for comfort for the Drug Cops. Nearly all the poppies produce alkaloids, some of which are rarely found outside this group of plants. But the substance known as opium is the fluid of the opium poppy, *Papaver somniferum*.

Normally this fluid is creamy white but can also be pink or even red. Pink poppy juice seems to come from the poppy at a certain stage in the plant's development and but doesn't seem to reflect much difference in chemical composition. Each seed head, if properly cared for, will deliver several grams of opium before it is done. "Exhausted" seed capsules are still good sources of opium alkaloids. A seed capsule that has been allowed to dry on the stalk without being "milked" for its opium has around twice as the total alkaloid content of those poppies that have been wounded two or more times during opium collection.

Fresh latex is bitter-tasting and the same consistency as fresh blood or a thin wood glue. It is generally smooth and homogeneous in texture, but some opium I've seen in films and photographs from poppies grown overseas has a lumpy appearance.

When the opium is exposed to air it quickly dries to a brown gum that can be rolled into balls or bars. Each region typically adopts a certain style for their opium; some fashion their opium into lens-shaped discs, bars, or even in the shape of fish. Opium shipped from India to China in the nineteenth century came in large chests filled with two-and-a-half-pound balls of opium nestled into little wooden compartments.

The discovery of opium's star alkaloid, morphine, led to some radical changes in medicine. But morphine is not the only alkaloid in opium, which contain at least 30, and probably closer to 40 chemicals, of which morphine, codeine, and thebaine are considered to be the most important. Of the three, morphine seems the most powerful ingredient in opium. Although it comprises only about ten percent of the weight of opium it is at least ten times stronger in many of its effects than opium by weight.

OPIUM IDENTIFICATION

OPIUM IDENTIFICATION IS AN ART FORM THAT'S BEEN IN USE FOR AGES. It's been necessary because, as a high-price, low-volume commodity, the temptation to cut it is great. Stepped-on opium was quite the problem for our forefathers whose records tell us the stuff has been adulterated with everything from feces to coffee. In larger quantities (as when nineteenth-century trading companies bought it by the chest or shipload) weight was increased by simply adding gravel.

These days opium identification is mostly a forensic matter as the opium trade (in the West at least) is now restricted to a few licensed firms who are not likely to be handed a chunk of cow manure for their money.

Although opium is not usually found on sale by street dealers, it sometimes surfaces there. More often it is purchased from a few people who have either smuggled it into the country after trips to Southeast Asia, or from people who have obtained it from poppies they grew themselves. As greater awareness of opium and cultivation of the opium poppy grows, and as law enforcement pinches off sales of dried poppies, it seems natural that opium will become more and more common. When and if that happens, some people will feel a need to identify it. Here's how:

Except for a short time after first exiting the capsule, opium is generally a very dark brown, almost black. It can range from a rubbery, Silly Putty-like consistency, to hard and brittle. It is also typical for it to have small flecks of dried plant material. Dirt, too, is commonly present in opium that has not been further prepared for either smoking or morphine extraction.

Fresh opium can be very sticky. This is especially true when dealing with the evaporation product from poppy tea, which can even stick to Teflon. If the opium you're examining doesn't have much of a smell, take a little piece of it and smash it between thumb and fingers and see if that doesn't release an odor, which should be fairly distinctive.

As opium ages, it tends to become brittle and to lose its odor, but brittle and relatively odorless opium isn't necessarily old. It might be that it has been prepared for smoking—a process that involves a kind of flame-drying procedure.

❖

It is not difficult to run simple tests on opium to verify what it really is, and even to give you an idea of its relative potency. For these tests, you'll need a few small glass test tubes. These can be substituted with small beakers or vials, or just about any other vessel made of glass—preferably of heat-resistant, borosilicate glass (Pyrex, Kimex, etc.). You will also need to buy or make one or more test reagents.

Other things you'll need are a couple of eyedroppers, the smaller the better, some empty glass vials or lens-like pieces of curved glass (or chemical-resistant plastics) called watch glasses, in which to perform the tests. Watch glasses are the better choice as they allow the sample to spread out better, allow a more accurate reading, and can be used for other purposes, such as evaporation.

You will also need a few chemicals to make your test solutions. These chemicals are available from chemical supply houses, including the smaller hobby suppliers, and will not raise any suspicion, as they are not used to make drugs. All of them use concentrated sulphuric acid, however, and for this you cannot substitute any of the brown-colored stuff sold as drain cleaner. As in any chemistry procedure, you're better off using the highest-quality chemicals you can. Substandard reagents can be worse than useless. Because these tests rely on noting a color change, your acid should be clear.

The first thing to do when testing opium is to drop a bit of it in water and watch what happens. Opium should not dissolve very much at all and leave a lot of junk floating around or at the bottom; this should be true even after heating. If you try to run this solution through a filter, you'll have an even better idea of how much of the stuff dissolved.

Black tar heroin, most commonly sold on the West Coast in the United States and imported from Mexico where it is manufactured, looks a lot like opium, but has some distinctive features that immediately set it apart. For one thing, tar heroin smells of vinegar from the acetic acid used to make it. For another, tar is quite water-soluble, while opium is not.

Now it's time to haul out your "Marquis reagent" alkaloid test. Since these tests can require time, you might want to set this up right away, performing the initial tests while giving the color test solution adequate time to do its thing.

For the color tests, use a piece of opium of about 100 milligrams in weight (one-tenth of a gram) for every one milliliter of water in your test tube. The water should be cold, no warmer than room temperature. Drop in the opium and note how it dissolves or doesn't dissolve. See if it gives off a smell. Let it settle and, using an eyedropper or better yet, run it through the improvised filter syringe, get a few drops of the liquid portion. Place this in another small test tube or suitable (but small) vessel made of glass so you can see what's going on. One drop is sufficient. To this add three or four drops of your Marquis reagent. Opium should turn the solution pink to purple after approximately one minute. The faster it does this, the better.

The next step requires a bit more of the original liquid obtained for your color tests. To this liquid add one drop of 2N HCl acid, along with as many as five drops of ferric sulphate solution. Opium should turn this all red. Further confirmation can be obtained by splitting up the results into two portions. To the first portion, add a couple drops of your HCl solution and warm it up (to around 100°–120°F). To the other, add a few drops of mercuric chloride solution.

In both of these tests, opium will give a persistent red color.

MORPHINE

AFTER ITS ISOLATION IN 1806 BY THE GERMAN DRUGGIST HANS WILLHELM Sertürner, Morphine became the standard by which opium and eventually all other painkillers were measured. Today morphine remains the standard of analgesia, thus we say that Dilaudid is seven to ten times as effective as morphine because it takes only a seventh or tenth as much to produce the same effects.

Morphine quickly usurped opium as a medicine. By the mid-1800s, morphine was being used in thousands of different medicines and used to treat almost any illness. The introduction of the hypodermic syringe made even stronger effects possible as direct injection into the bloodstream bypassed the liver where much of morphine is metabolized into other products.

Experiments with the yellowish powdered alkaloid led to the invention of heroin, made by a fairly straightforward process of acetylation of morphine. Although C.M.E. Wright first discovered heroin in 1874 at St. Mary's Hospital in London, England, he shelved the experiment. Heroin was invented again, but this time also seriously developed by chemists at the Bayer company in Germany—the same chemists who invented aspirin just the year before. Heroin was seen mostly as a cough remedy in the beginning and heroin cough lozenges became big sellers.

Heroin was the first of a long line of semi-synthetic opiates derived by screwing around with the morphine molecule. More semi-synthetics have been created from codeine and thebaine. Thebaine presents us with an interesting phenomenon: by itself it has no narcotic properties; if anything it is a stimulant, even a convulsant, and now the starting material for oxycodone. Thebaine has also served as the basis for hundreds of new drugs known as Bentley Compounds (after their inventer K.W. Bentley). One of these compounds is the drug etorphine, which is 1,000 to 3,000 times more powerful than morphine. As a drug, a therapeutic dose of etorphine is measured in micrograms and is by weight one of the strongest drugs in the world, stronger even than LSD-25. Today it sees its most famous use as a big game tranquilizer—shot from an air rifle, an etorphine dart brings down charging rhinos or elephants within a minute or two. When the technicians are finished with the animal they use another Bentley compound that displaces the etorphine and blocks it.

Another interesting characteristic of etorphine and related alkaloids (buprenorphine is one) is their possibilities in treating opiate addiction. Etorphine alkaloids seem to suppress withdrawal symptoms almost completely. They also provide a fairly high level of pain relief with nothing near the addiction liability. In some experiments, test animals have been given daily doses of etorphine over long periods of time and failed to show signs of physical dependence

OPIUM PERFUME, THE REAL THING

THE BEST-SELLING PERFUME CALLED "OPIUM" DOESN'T SMELL MUCH LIKE opium at all. For those who insist on the real thing there is an answer, courtesy of a merry band of smell scientists at the Institute of Pharmaceutical Chemistry, University of Vienna, Austria.

Using a method known as "headspace technology," which is used to capture and identify the various components of a particular scent (and really is used in the perfume industry to duplicate certain elusive odors to be mixed into their products), the guys analyzed a chunk of "medicinal opium."

After running the chunk through a few sophisticated mechanical and chemical tests (one of which is called "GC-sniffing") they compared their findings with the sensitive nose of a trained police dog. The results?

Opium's smell, they discovered, is composed of more than 70 identifiable components. But opium's characteristic scent is attributable to only one class of chemicals known as pyrazines. Using some of these components they were able to whip up a passable fake opium scent. In case you have your own perfumer and want to smell like a chunk of medicinal opium, tell him what the scientists discovered, namely that:

The synthetic mixture of 2-methyl-, 2,5-, and 2,6-dimethylpyrazine with 2-methoxy-3-isopropyl- and 2-methoxy-3-isobutylpyrazine was found to represent the original opium odour quite well.

source:

• *Planta Medica* 60: 181–183 (1994)

• *Headspace Constituents of Opium* by Buchbauer G, Nikiforov A, Remberg B

Another alkaloid component of opium, papaverine, has a rather interesting use: when injected into the base of a penis, it causes an erection! This treatment has obvious benefits for men suffering from impotence. Papaverine was also one of the first reliable drugs used to lower blood pressure. Today's blood pressure medication Verapamil is derived from the alkaloid.

Noscapine (a.k.a. narcotine, even though it has no narcotic properties) has been used for decades in Japan and other countries in place of codeine as a cough remedy, but not in the United States. The alkaloid may soon find its way into the U.S. market, however, since it was recently discovered to be surprisingly effective at killing cancer cells. Graduate student Keqiang Ye of Emory University selected noscapine as his compound in experiments assigned to him by his professor, Dr. Harrish Joshi. The two scientists injected mice with human breast cancer cells, which quickly produced large, dense tumors. But the administration of noscapine reduced the tumors almost as quickly as they appeared. Within three weeks, 80% of the tumors had been destroyed.

The mysteries of etorphine, noscapine or papaverine, along with the actions of endorphins clearly suggest that opium is much more than just a source of morphine.

PHARMACOKINETICS AND PHARMACOLOGY OF OPIATES

NOT ALL OPIATES OR OPIOIDS ARE ALIKE. THE MANY ALKALOID DRUGS derived from opium and the many more synthetic and semi-synthetic opioid drugs inspired by those alkaloids all have differing mechanisms of action to produce different effects. Some of these effects are clinically very important. One may cause less respiratory depression without any reduction in analgesia, another may cause bizarre nightmares but have a lower addiction liability, and of course, duration of action is the biggest difference between an analgesic used during surgery and the analgesic chosen to keep the patient pain-free while he recovers from that surgery.

In this way, opioid drugs are similar to enkephalins and endorphins, the internal opioids produced by the body. These substances, too, produce different effects, mostly by binding at one or more of numerous opioid receptors.

Morphine remains the cornerstone of opiate science. The analgesic effects of codeine are thought to come from the morphine the liver metabolizes from codeine. Heroin, in fact, turns out to be just a variation on the morphine molecule, which allows the drug to deliver morphine in far larger quantities to the brain than is naturally possible. Within 15 minutes of a dose of heroin, all of it has been converted to morphine and morphine metabolites. In fact, one of the drawbacks to both morphine and heroin are their very short periods of action: no more than six hours and usually far less. This means a user needs to take a dose of morphine several times a day, whether to control pain or to maintain an addiction.

So heroin is just as fast-acting as morphine but packs a much larger punch.

OPIOID DRUGS

NALOXONE: MARKETED UNDER THE NAME "NARCAN," THIS IS THE CLASSIC pure opiate antagonist, and its introduction has saved countless lives from opiate overdoses. Naloxone has a very strong affinity for opiate receptors and because of this and its rapid onset of action, an injection of naloxone can almost instantly bring a dying OD victim back to life. In fact, the stuff works so well emergency medical personnel report that a typical reaction from the patient is marked irritation. As soon as their eyes open they begin cursing at the lifesaver! In the victim's defense, he or she rarely knows how close to dying they were. All they know is one moment they were feeling lovely and the next moment they were shocked back into a world where they were no longer high, but in a hurt. With all that naloxone blocking their receptors, they are thrown into instant withdrawal.

NALTREXONE: A close relative of naloxone, naltrexone is another opiate antagonist, once known as "Trexan," but now manufactured and sold by Dupont Merk under the happier-sounding name Revia. It has a slower onset of action but a much longer duration and, while it isn't the drug of choice for it, it has been used to reverse overdose like naloxone.

Its more typical use is to maintain opiate addicts once they have gotten clean. A relatively small dose of the drug, taken in pill form, effectively blocks even large amounts of heroin or other opiate agonists for 24 hours and longer. However, it is not without its dangers. Should a dedicated junkie attempt to overcome the blockade, he or she can come seriously close to a fatal overdose. Another drawback occurs when a patient on Revia is injured or otherwise requires pain medication the Revia will block. This situation can be treated by judicious doses of a strong opiate such as Dilaudid, but anyone taking the drug should perhaps wear a warning bracelet like people with allergies to bee stings wear.

And, of course, the drug should never be taken by anyone still taking opiate drugs. Even small amounts will send that person into an exquisitely uncomfortable, even potentially fatal, withdrawal.

Although it is supposed to reduce cravings in opiate addicts, almost no one using the drug reports this effect. Junkies using Revia never really get used to taking the drug because of the discomfort it causes.

The most interesting and exciting use for Revia has been to control alcoholism. Perhaps by the same system that allows morphine to substitute for alcohol, Revia has been shown to reduce craving for booze and got FDA's approval for that use in early 1995. The drug may have a competitor in "methylnaltrexone," which is made by Jansson.

DEXTROMETHORPHAN: This is the stuff found in "DM" cough syrups sold over the counter as a substitute for codeine. A glance at its molecular structure shows how similar it is to other opioid drugs, although it does not bind at any of the opiate receptor sites. Instead, it exerts its anti-cough action by an anti-convulsant mechanism inhibiting the certain neurotransmissions, especially at the N methyl D aspartate (NMDA) receptor. Another well-known drug with this action is the disassociative anesthetic ketamine.

In recent years, DM and its O-demethylated metabolite, the phencyclidine-like dextrorphan (DXO), have been the subjects of intense study for their neuroprotective properties. DM, it seems, can reduce brain and nerve damage caused by stroke, head injuries and the like. It has even been investigated as a defense against nerve gas, in tests carried out by the U.S. Army.

Like ketamine, DM has been shown to reduce the buildup of tolerance to morphine and to lessen the symptoms of inflammatory-type pain and the discomfort of withdrawal in opiate addicts. These findings, along with DM's long record of safety in uses of all types in humans means we'll probably be seeing some good things from it.

TRAMADOL in solution is used in Taiwan to help patients undergoing heroin withdrawal.

MEPEREDINE (pethidine): Otherwise known as Demerol, this is a real popular pre-op drug and is often used in place of codeine for pain relief in hospitals. Invented by the Germans in 1939, it was the first totally synthetic opiate and has only one-sixth the strength of morphine. Unlike morphine, however, this stuff is neurotoxic and overdoses can easily kill or permanently damage you. It also doesn't seem to feel as good as natural opiates and is jeered at by junkies as "Dummy Oil." But its main feature, rapid onset, makes it still the weapon of choice for in-hospital post-operative pain and for certain diagnostic procedures performed in hospitals. Like heroin, meperidine is lipophilic (fat-soluble) and so, where an epidural injection of morphine takes three hours to reach peak concentrations in areas around the brainstem, meperidine's peak occurs within 30 to 60 minutes. In the world of illicit drugs, analogs of meperedine developed by clandestine chemists have proven dangerous, causing instant and permanent Parkinson's disease in some users.

FENTANYL: This drug is in the same class as meperidine but is at least 50 times more potent than morphine, so it is quite effective at relieving pain. It also has the advantage of being absorbable through the skin and transdermal patches containing fentanyl are often used for as much as three days analgesia.

One problem with fentanyl occurs on the street where it is sometimes mixed into heroin to beef up a weak product. It doesn't take more than a speck or two to make the resulting product lethal and hundreds of heroin addicts have been killed by it. Heroin containing fentanyl is sometimes called "China White," and erroneously referred to in news stories as a kind of super-heroin.

HYDROCODONE: This is the schedule III drug widely used in cough syrups and pain killers for moderate to severe pain, such as in tooth extractions, kidney stones and the like. Hydrocodone (trade name: Vicodin) was first prepared in 1920 by German chemists Mannich and Lowenheim. It has a chemical structure very similar to codeine and, like codeine, it survives heavy metabolism by the liver, and thus maintains considerable oral potency.

One interesting feature of hydrocodone is that it is eliminated from the system in the form of hydromorphone (see Dilaudid). Of course, the production of hydromorphone is dependent on the Cytochrome P450 2D6 (CYP2D6) enzyme that performs the same sort of O-demethylation that makes codeine into morphine. Studies have shown the ability to perform this transformation has a lot to do with the subjective liking of the drug.

As the only truly effective relief for moderate to severe pain in the Schedule III category, hydrocodone is a popular drug indeed. In December 1995, a Reuters market report showed hydrocodone/acetaminophen products had been growing at 20% per year for the previous four years!

Another interesting thing about hydrocodone is the intensity of brand loyalty among its fans, including pharmacists. Devotees of one brand or another (especially of Vicodin) swear there is a difference. In 1995, a Ph.D. candidate in pharmacology performed some solubility experiments among brands of hydrocodone and found a marked difference in availability curves. It is possible that the rate of absorption, mediated by the fillers and binders in a particular brand, are responsible for this palpable difference.

OXYCODONE: This is the stuff in Tylox, Percocet, and Percodan. Oxycodone seems to be a popular pill among the Hollywood set who are forever getting addicted to it, blaming their personal problems on it, then kicking at swank recovery farms. It is made from thebaine. Quite powerful. It, too, has its devotees, much like hydrocodone.

PENTAZOCINE: This interesting synthetic opiate was once gleefully abused almost exclusively by health-care professionals. Mixed with an antihistamine called tripelennamine, the combo was known as "Ts and Blues" and said to be a lot like heroin in its effect. Today, the antihistamine is available in Canada as an over-the-counter pill called Pyribenzamine. As a painkiller it's only half as strong as morphine and its reformulation now includes a narcotic antagonist to prevent users from getting off on it. There is, however, a formulation of the drug available without any naloxone, called Talacen. Pharmacokinetically, pentazocine possesses both agonist and antagonist properties, a group of opioids sometimes selected for pain relief because they are supposedly less liable to be abused and to cause the dreaded addiction. This sort of chemical compound, known as a "quinoline," can also be hallucinogenic. Pentazocine doesn't usually cause hallucinations, but a not-uncommon side effect is nightmares, especially in old people.

HYDROMORPHONE: This is the famous Dilaudid, as much as ten times stronger than morphine and, like heroin, derived from the morphine molecule. Although this is the drug that killed one of our heroes in the movie *Drugstore Cowboy*, it is not usually associated with death. Notice the word "laudanum" hiding in the name Dilaudid?

LOPERAMIDE: This is the stuff in Imodium AD and it's not supposed to get you high, although some people feel a mild euphoria from it. I include it here because it functions as a kind of poor man's methadone. In larger than normal doses, this stuff can halt some of the worst opium withdrawal symptoms. It has been proven to stop withdrawal symptoms in morphine-dependent monkeys. In humans it does the same thing and could be used by junkies as an OTC alternative to government-supplied and government-monitored methadone. It's cheaper, too. The liquid form of loperamide absorbs better and faster than the pill form and both have a half-life of almost 11 hours.

METHADONE: Now this is an interesting synthetic. It is an ingenious creation of chemistry, and because of its use as a government approved heroin substitute, it is surrounded by all kinds of cultural baggage—including the yarn that it was once named after Adolf Hitler. Today it is used for maintaining junkies so they'll stay away from heroin. It has also been used as a pain killer for cancer patients because, unlike morphine, it is a long-lasting analgesic. Its half-life can be as much as 50 hours. Another compound related to methadone, called levo-alphaacetylmethadol (LAAM), is even longer-lasting. LAAM's effects go on for anywhere from 48 to 72 hours.

Methadone was invented by the Germans during the second World War as a replacement for morphine when supplies of opium from Turkey were interrupted.

The Adolf Hitler legend comes from the fact that the drug was called Dolophine. Some people have leaped to the conclusion that this was in honor of Adolf Hitler (Dolophine coming from a contraction of "Adolfaphine" or something like that). But the name seems to have been coined much later by the American drug firm Eli Lilly, which probably derived it from the Latin "dolor" for pain.

CH_3CH_2C — C — CH_2 — CH — N — CH_3 / CH_3

‖
O

CH_3

METHADONE MOLECULE

HOW METHADONE GOT TO AMERICA

AFTER THE WAR A TEAM OF AMERICAN SCIENTISTS WERE ROOTING AROUND in the laboratories of I.G. Farben in Elberfeld, Germany, systematically cataloging and describing whatever they found. One of the things they found was Analgesic #10820, or Amidone. When the team's civilian leader, Dr. Irvin C. Kleiderer, got back stateside he quickly went to work for Eli Lilly & Co., the pharmaceutical firm in Indianapolis, IN. Soon Lilly was producing the new drug, calling it Dolophine.

Methadone is also an agonist, like heroin, morphine or any other, but the way it relieves the pain of opiate withdrawal without producing much of a high is not through antagonism. Methadone prevents drugs like heroin from occupying the receptors because its affinity for the receptor is greater. At the same time, however, it does not produce the same level of stimulation as heroin so the user does not get the same sort of high obtainable from heroin or morphine.

It is this effect, coupled with its long half-life, that means opiate addicts can take methadone just once a day and go about their business without discomfort and without getting high... or at least as high.

Propoxyphene: From methadone, Lilly developed a highly successful synthetic opiate called propoxyphene—the active ingredient in Darvon and Darvocet. Both of these pills have been fantastically popular pain relievers although they supposedly have no more analgesic power than aspirin. However, probably because of its pleasurable opiate side effects, it is perceived as being much stronger. Patients clearly prefer it to plain aspirin. Like methadone, Darvocet is only a mild narcotic agonist and has been used to maintain junkies just like methadone. ❖

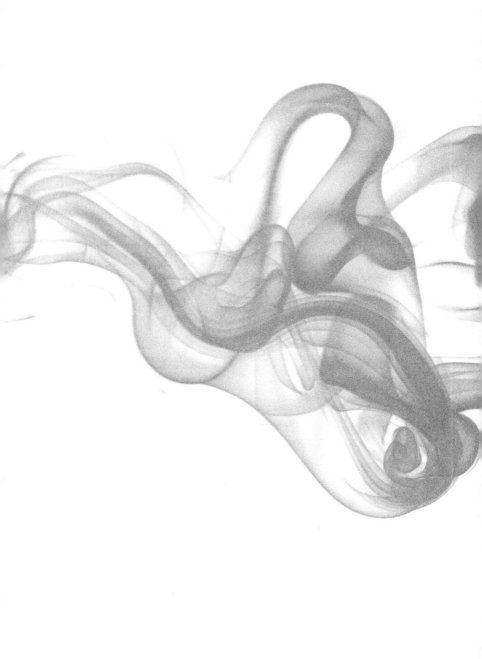

CHAPTER 6
ENDORPHINS

The ying-su is a good plant to have. It is called ying because, though small, it is shaped like a fine vase; it is called su because the little seeds look like those of millet. When first growing it maybe eaten like the vegetables of spring. When ground, the seeds and head yield a sap like cow's milk: when boiled, this becomes a drink fit for Buddha. Old men whose powers have decayed, who have little appetite, who when they eat meat cannot digest it and when they eat vegetables cannot distinguish their flavor, should take this drink.

Use a willow mallet and stone basin to beat it. Boil it in water sweetened with honey. It does good to the mouth and the throat. It restores tranquility to the lungs and nourishes the stomach.

For three years now the door has been closed. I have gone nowhere and come back from nowhere. I see here the hermit of the shade and the long-robed priest: when they sit opposite I forget to speak. Then I have but to drink a cup of poppy nectar. I laugh. I am happy. I have come to Ying-ch'uan, and am wandering the banks of the river there. I am climbing the slopes of the Lu mountain of the far west.

— Su Che, early Tang Dynasty —

T'S ONE THING TO SPEAK OF "WALKING THROUGH SILK" AND another to chatter away about polypeptide chains and kappa receptors. It may not be as poetic, but an understanding of opium is impossible without looking at what we have learned about its pharmacology.

So far, we have only scratched the surface. Most experiments on opiate receptors have been done using a single alkaloid of opium and carefully observing its action. If that alkaloid happened to be morphine then we have only 38 other chemicals to look at. If it's methadone then all bets are off. It's difficult to assess what methadone studies tell us. Methadone never occurs in nature and is the product of some brilliant minds trying to make a morphine substitute.

Experiments using any of the myriad semi-synthetic opiates available give us data of the rawest sort. Information obtained by such experiments doesn't tell us a lot about poppy juice. Studies on the chemical actions of heroin are a sideways (and narrow) approach to investigating the vastly more complicated actions of something like opium.

Nevertheless, we've found out a lot about endorphins.

❖

Endorphins have come into common parlance as the chemicals responsible for the famous "runner's high." It is generally understood that the body produces endorphins as a response to stress, particularly physical pain. One of the effects of these endorphins is a mild euphoria along with analgesia. People getting tattoos also report a kind of high they get from repeated jabs with a needle.

That endorphins are very powerful is borne out by the way many runners become addicted to their sport. If an addicted runner cannot run at least a few miles a day he may become depressed and eventually start to feel sick, the withdrawal effects from his running fix.

The word endorphin comes from mashing together the words "endo" (Greek for within or inside) and "morphine." But endorphins are far more complicated and much subtler than simply "head-morphine."

Although the existence of opiate receptors had been theorized for a long while, it was not until 1973 that an opiate receptor was scientifically identified—and then at least three major laboratories around the world happened to discover it almost exactly at the same time.

The announcements—by Candace Pert and her professor Solomon Snyder at Johns Hopkins University, Eric Simon at the New York Medical Center, and Lars Terenius at Uppsala, Sweden, all came nearly simultaneously. Bad news for the professors but great news for opiate buffs since their work was, in effect, already tested and verified three times over.

THE BRAIN'S OPIUM

It is simplistic to view endorphins as merely the brain's version of morphine. For one thing, morphine is not a protein. It fits into opiate receptors like a peptide chain but is not made from amino acids like endorphins. Because endorphins are made up of chains of amino acids called peptides and peptides form proteins, permutations on this theme are legion. These chemical keys, for all their exacting scientific names, fit into more than one receptor. And they are all related to the same three parent molecules produced in three different places in the brain and nervous system.

So the brain produces a slew of related substances called endorphins that come from three precursor chemicals elaborated and excreted from various parts of the brain and all playing a role in perceptions of pain and mood. The first endorphin to be identified was called enkephalin (from Greek "inside the head") but when it became apparent it was not the only endorphin it got renamed met-enkephalin, The next was dubbed leu-enkephalin due to a characteristic amino acid in its chain.

More digging turned up substances far more powerful than these enkephalins (and far more powerful than plain morphine). One was dubbed dynorphin (from Greek again, meaning "power"). Soon, 11 distinct endorphins from three families had been described. Chief among these was beta-endorphin, a natural opiate that has been shown to accompany pregnancy in increasing amounts right up until birth is completed. Two days later, it's gone. Unexpectedly, a relationship to pain suppression on behalf of the mother could not be established. It is now thought that the beta-endorphins so prominent during pregnancy are for the benefit of the fetus.

"It's wild speculation," said Candace Pert on an episode of *Nova*, "but it's very interesting to think about a fetus floating around with its opiate receptors loaded with endogenous endorphins. A fetus in that position would be sleepy, would be relaxed. Its gastrointestinal motility would be suppressed, would be calm. It wouldn't breathe; we don't want it to breathe when it's in the uterus surrounded by liquid; we want it to breathe when it comes out. It's fascinating... to think about the fetus in this blissful prenatal state medicated by beta-endorphin."

No wonder babies bawl so furiously upon being yanked from the womb. The shock of birth—expelled from this dreamy, dark paradise to smack the cold air in the harsh, bright world—must be horrific! The party is most certainly over for the baby as he hacks fluid from his lungs and draws his first dry breath.

The stolen bliss of prenatal existence is a compelling explanation for why we naturally seek the "fetal position" when faced with pain or adversity. It is even possible that such a position itself stimulates the production of endorphins. The same is true of physical contact, especially caressing. It could very well be that a cat's contented purr is a result of these endogenous opiates. This kind of chemistry blurs the distinction between matter and thought. Feelings are chemical reactions and chemical reactions, in turn, are feelings.

Reality can, to an extent, be understood in terms of chemicals and receptors.

MORE THAN JUST A PASSEL OF ENDORPHINS

OPIATES BLURRED THE LINE BETWEEN PLANT ALKALOID AND DRUG, and then further blurred the demarcations between exogenous plant alkaloid and more "natural" endorphins when it was discovered that all mammals—humans included—manufacture morphine and other opium alkaloids. The body's morphine, it turns out, is morphine!

Perhaps it's time to ditch our artificial classifications and realize that opiates, opioids, endorphins and enkephalins are all related and not the exclusive province of plants or animals. All through the history of opium chemistry we are confronted with the frequent need to revise the neat lines we draw while categorizing all these chemicals. At one time it was stated with certitude that morphine—or some other opium alkaloid — was produced only in *Papaver somniferum*. Even as the statement was made there was evidence of exceptions to this apparent rule.

The system of brain opiates and their receptors is far more complex than a simple deadening of a nerve or a lift of the spirits. Likewise, opium is more than super-aspirin. Endorphins are best viewed as a group of chemicals, and are better compared to opium as a whole than to any single opium derivative. Brains do not excrete just one endorphin at a time and endorphins do not simply act like morphine alone. The range of effects of both endorphins and opium is wide and has yet to be fully understood. It may turn out that opium—and not a mixture of isolated substances from opium—resembles the whole of the brain's endorphin system.

The fundamental roles played by endorphins suggest that these chemicals are essential not only for basic survival, but also play a big part in our perceptions of reality as well as the prevention of disease.

The recent use of codeine to treat narcolepsy runs completely against most accepted medical understandings of opiates. Previously, this disease has been treated only with very powerful stimulants like dextroamphetamine. Codeine was considered a depressant, more likely to cause than prevent sleep. Opium's alkaloids are obviously more complex than we thought.

Morphine and codeine were both used to treat diabetes even after the advent of insulin. Opioids may still have a role to play in the management of this condition.

There is also the demonstrated effect opiates have on the body's immune system. Just as changes in the molecule's structure are associated with changes in analgesia, the immune system is also influenced by similar alterations. Some opiates, such as morphine or heroin, reduce the activity of the immune system, while others—oxycodone for example—have no effect on the same system.

❖

The opiates' relationship to the immune system only broadens the therapeutic value of these drugs. Just as a side effect like drowsiness can be desirable from a treatment point of view, it is sometimes desirable to dial down the body's immune response. The old junkie's claim that his opiate use protects him against disease doesn't seem like such a wild claim.

Casual observation of junkies also supports this theory. When an opiate addict is suddenly deprived of dope, the symptoms of opiate withdrawal are predictable and revealing: runny nose, exhaustion, vomiting, fever, and aching muscles. In other words, the same symptoms as accompany the flu.

While amphetamines, alcohol, or cocaine might slowly (or quickly) destroy a user's body, opium and even most of its semi-synthetic derivatives, including heroin, do not cause tissue or nerve damage. The ugly, collapsed veins of a street junkie's arms, legs, neck (or anyplace else) are caused by the use of dirty needles and the noxious adulterants of illicit drugs, not opiates themselves. Rich heroin users, who can afford to shoot either high-quality heroin or pharmaceutical opiates, are just as pudgy and pink as their cleanest-living neighbor.

Folks can ingest opium on a daily basis for decades without suffering physical harm as a result of it. As long has they continue to eat well and observe normal hygiene, the worst thing that happens would be constipation. Thomas de Quincey, author of *Confessions of an English Opium Eater*, was addicted to the drug for a half-century, dying at the age of 74. William S. Burroughs, an unrepentant junkie throughout most of his life, unhesitatingly credited his use of opiates for his longevity.

THE DAPPER PIPIE

IN THE EARLY PART OF THIS CENTURY WHEN OPIUM USE WAS ENJOYING its last days of popularity in America, opium was considered a status drug. Users donned silk pajamas and lounged on large mattresses while inhaling long drags of opium smoke. Opium was inexpensive and posed no financial hardship on the partiers. Opium's effects are subtle and tranquil, so opium parties did not attract police attention or outrage the neighbors.

Opium smokers prided themselves on their civilized manners, and looked down on heroin users. As drug enforcement became harsher, bulky, hard-to-smuggle opium lost out to the far more powerful heroin. The Jewish mobsters who supplied opium began to lose out to the Italians who specialized in heroin.

Opium disappeared in the 1940s and people soon found themselves at the mercy of an expensive drug they had to inject. In their book *Addicts Who Survived*, authors David Courtwright, Herman Joseph, and Don Des Jarlais interviewed elderly people enrolled in methadone programs to compile their oral history of narcotic use in America, 1923–1965.

The hophead codgers spoke wistfully of the good old days when opium was abundant and as socially acceptable as drinking alcohol. Most continued using opium until the 1940s, when it was replaced by morphine or heroin. Addicted to opiates, they switched to the semi-synthetics and went from jaunty ladies and gents to pathetic and socially illicit junkies. The following quote from a 76-year-old woman (now enrolled in a methadone program) typifies the sharp distinctions made between a heroin user and an opium smoker.

There's nothing like a pipie (opium smoker). They kept themselves immaculate—dresses, furs. I had a diamond, black mink coat. I had a mink stole, a Persian stole—whatever fur was, I had it because you wanted to look good. Nobody even knew I was a pipie. When people found out I was a pipie, they couldn't believe it. Instead of a pipie, they said I was a junkie already—which I never was, then. There was a million times difference between heroin and opium users, a million times.

When I became a junkie, I lost my life. ❖

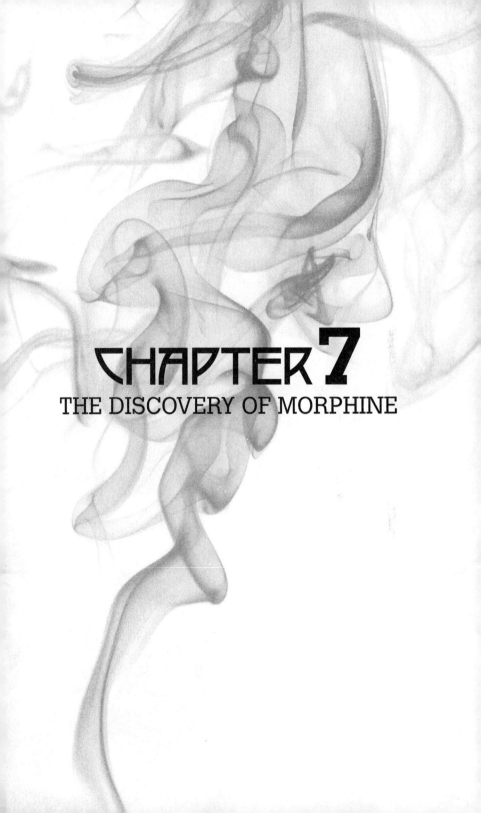

CHAPTER 7
THE DISCOVERY OF MORPHINE

Ah, pierce me 100 times with your needles fine and I will thank you 100 times, Saint Morphine, you who Aeseulapus has made a God.

— Jules Verne —

MORPHINE MOLECULE

OPIUM FITS UNCANNILY WELL INTO THE BRAIN. The ease with which opioid chemicals are interchanged with chemicals needed and manufactured by the body has led to the suspicion that poppies were placed here on earth for the express purpose of providing opium—a kind of neural nutrient. Fascination with opium's effectiveness helped spread its use in medicine. It also motivated European man to take it apart and see what made it tick.

It was this investigation into opium that caused a fundamental change in the practice of pharmacology in the Western world, bringing us along a path we still follow today. For one thing, the isolation of morphine from opium gave us the pharmacologic concept of "the active ingredient."

Prior to the middle of the nineteenth century, plants, and to some extent, animal and mineral products, formed the basis of all medicines. Foxglove tea was used successfully to treat congestive heart failure. Willow bark was used as an analgesic. And opium was used to treat almost anything. One of the biggest reasons for the widespread use of opium was that it worked well and predictably. It controlled pain. It could stop coughing, promote sleep, increase appetite, relieve melancholy and halt diarrhea. In contrast to a lot of other nostrums, opium had broad therapeutic value and was the workhorse of medicine.

THEN CAME MORPHINE.

MORPHINE WAS DISCOVERED IN 1806 WHEN A GERMAN SCIENTIST, HANS Sertürmer, isolated the principal alkaloid in opium and declared morphine the thing that made opium work. By using pure morphine (named after the Greek god of sleep, Morpheus) doctors could attack pain with more devastating effect than opium alone could provide. With the invention in 1853 of the hypodermic syringe, morphine's fate was sealed. It became a certified miracle. Physicians became gods.

An injection of morphine could instantly erase the most horrible suffering. Freedom from pain brought endless gratitude from patients. Opium worked too slowly to do this, could not be injected.

With morphine it became possible to know the precise strength of a dose. Science enabled the doctor to calibrate nature. Science had triumphed, unlocked the mysteries of opium.

Morphine was the first member of a new category of chemical compound: the alkaloid. The identification of alkaloids opened up a frontier in pharmaceutical chemistry that soon dominated the field. As scientists investigated other medicinal plants, they hit a jackpot of powerful drug substances. Cocaine, strychnine, mescaline, quinine, reserpine, berberine, caffeine and the rest of a long list of "active ingredients" followed close behind.

THE POPPY WAS A GIFT THAT KEEP ON GIVING.

Further investigation into opium turned up still more alkaloids of varying degrees of importance. Codeine's ability to still coughs was noted and logged. There was no turning back from the age of "the active ingredient." With morphine, plant medicines began to be seen as crude and homely. Soon, alkaloids and other substances extracted from plants were the order of the day. No more belladonna for cramps; now physicians used its derivative, atropine. Foxglove yielded digitalis; quinine was extracted from willow bark.

New folk remedies gave way to purified forms of their active ingredients. Natural products from hemlock to animal testicles were ground up, bathed in acids, heated, evaporated, electrocuted, and dried, until they gave up their "spirits" to the new medicine.

The isolation of morphine marked a sea change as chemists began churning out compounds that promised an end to all sorts of human misery. Even dread diseases like syphilis and rabies started to crack under the onslaught. Faith in medicine and doctors soared, while fear of disease began to retreat. Fantastic dreams of birth control pills and medicines to stop infection were on the horizon. The future gleamed and plant medicines were left behind for primitive folk who knew no better.

Medicine was created that could kill cancer cells or release schizophrenics from their private hells. Diabetics started to live decades longer and the number of truly active drugs mushroomed.

Scientists kept tinkering with morphine, creating semi-synthetic versions of the molecule, like heroin. When heroin came on the scene in 1898 it was considered better than morphine because it was far stronger. By adding two acetyl groups to the morphine molecule, chemists created a brand new substance capable of delivering at least twice the amount of morphine to the brain. Later developments eventually brought us synthesized molecules having as much as 3,000 times the pain-killing power of morphine. An amount of etorphine measured in millionths of a gram packs the same analgesic punch as a hundred pounds of opium.

Research into opiate synthesis continues today but opium is no longer a subject of much scientific interest. By the beginning of the twentieth century, opium (though far better understood and described in a technical sense than ever before) was becoming seen as old-fashioned. Within a decade it had become a symbol of depravity and crime, where it remains today in the popular mind—an illegal and dangerous drug that might just pervert your daughter into fucking a Chinaman. Opium established another first in America when, in 1915, it became the country's first illegal drug.

THE PAIN OF MORPHINE
SCIENCE AND POLITICS

NOT ALL SCIENTIFIC INQUIRY LED US TO SUCH DUBIOUS PRIZES AS morphine—an amazing drug for sure, but definitely not the "spirit of opium." It wasn't long before people began to explore the why and how of these new drugs, leading to still more new compounds. This increase of knowledge led to exponentially more knowledge (and bewilderment, too). Once an understanding of antibiotics was attained, it became easier to conceive of, then develop, new ones. But a better understanding of disease revealed the concept to be more complex than ever before. New diseases and syndromes were discovered, and new ideas about how an illness is acquired competed with concepts that had served physicians for hundreds of years.

On a political level, too, medicine underwent a transformation. Once an art form associated with quasi-magical, religious, or monkish academic pursuit of knowledge for its own sake, medicine became government territory. In the United States—beyond laws circumscribing fraud or theft—there had been no real regulation of medicine or of who got to call themselves a physician. Those few laws that were passed to regulate medicine were usually repealed.

By the end of the nineteenth century this had changed radically. Laws regulating the practice of medicine were in effect all over the country. Soon, regulations dictated what could be sold as medicine and provided criminal penalties for those who disobeyed (or disagreed and acted on it). By 1920, medicine was entirely the government's business, and physicians were controlled by a group no one had heard of at the turn of the century: The American Medical Association.

Early in the struggle over control of medicine, the nascent AMA had thrown its lot in with the government in the conflict over who would exert control over the use of opiates, and whether the Harrison Act represented an improper government intrusion into private life. Although the AMA was apparently rewarded for its choice (becoming a de facto representative of the government's policies), the victory was bittersweet.

Almost immediately after the Harrison Act came into effect, government agents started locking up physicians for violating its restrictions on "non-medical" prescribing. Drugs, medicines, were no longer the property of the people. They were now regulated by employees of government agencies who anointed the legitimacy of drugs. It's ironic that Hans Sertürner's work with morphine, which set off such an avalanche of scientific advances, would be so illegal today that the young chemist would be sentenced to a lifetime in prison. A century after his discovery, morphine had already shifted in public perception from scientific and medical miracle to a sort of evil genie in a bottle viewed with fear—an evil foisted upon mankind by his weakness in the face of pain.

❖

By the 1960s, advancements in neurology and psychiatric pharmacology revealed the existence of brain chemicals, which led to the concept of receptors within the brain for these chemicals. The body had already been understood as a mechanical and hydraulic system. Now the brain, too, was a machine full of little switches operated by electricity and chemical reactions.

Some of the switches appeared to operate when certain chemicals fit specific receptors like a key in a lock. Instead of gross medication of a problem, it seemed possible to begin crafting drugs that could do just one thing and one thing only.

Such a drug would be like Cinderella's glass slipper. Perfect. Specific. Ultra-refined. Only one thing was missing to complete the picture: there had to be proof these receptors existed, then the intensive work of learning how they worked could begin.

Because of research done into the mechanisms of opiates, discoveries of other types of neuroreceptors had been made. For instance, we now know that diazepam (Valium) and its many similar compounds called benzodiazepines, produce their anxiety relief, muscle relaxation, and other effects by stimulating specific benzodiazepine receptors in the human brain.

Brain chemicals synthesized from proteins were recognized as the engines of thought, even feelings. Studies led to chemicals that stimulated or blocked reactions at receptor sites to achieve a desired physiological response. This in turn affected psychological responses, too. The latest antidepressants work at specific serotonin receptor sites (each with its own name and number) to eradicate sadness and fear. Ulcer medications, antagonists, operate on the same principle of receptor sites and chemicals that block, rather than stimulate.

And this same line of enquiry gave us Prozac and Tagamet, which led us right back to opium. Specifically it leads us to polypeptide chains of amino acids of stunning construction known as endorphins.

❖

Discoveries in endorphin chemistry failed to answer the larger question, which only became more nagging. Just how is it that morphine—and all the other opioid substances found in nature or whipped up in a laboratory beaker—fit into these receptors that were obviously not meant for them? If plant alkaloids were so inferior, how was it they worked at all? Did man and poppy somehow co-evolve?

Since the early '70s, and especially in the past decade, the sharp line between people and poppies has blurred again. For one thing morphine was discovered in the human brain, and produced there for God knows what reason. This miraculous alkaloid was supposed to come from a plant, and from just one plant at that. Careful study has shown the presence of morphine in a lot more plants than the opium poppy, and in a lot more living things than plants.

Morphine, it turns out, is everywhere. It's been found in rat livers, cow's milk, and even worms. Both plant and mammal manufacture morphine from amino acids, usually from tyrosine. From tyrosine the substance morphs and flips and snaps bonds and double bonds into rings, while exchanging atoms with other nearby building materials. Morphine may be more widespread than we think. Some plants that don't make it now could probably be bred to do it in short order. Consider this: when given an injection of codeine, the tobacco plant will turn it into morphine, too.

At present, opium science has reached a sort of nexus. Endorphins (made of amino acids hooked together) and opium alkaloids (made from amino acids) seem to do essentially the same things in essentially the same places. Biochemists can now create synthetic endorphins and even hybrids of amino acid chains and alkaloidal fragments that have opiate-like effects.

MORPHINE AND HEROIN

IN TERMS OF DIFFICULTY, THE PROCESS OF GETTING MORPHINE FROM opium and then turning it into heroin is comparable to making homemade wine or beer. In both cases the procedure can be carried out by a novice carefully following a recipe, and chances are good he'll get a decent product. But there is also a certain art to doing it well that goes beyond technical proficiency; improvement is gained from experience.

Since heroin is made from morphine and morphine must first be obtained from opium, the process of making heroin from opium consists of two distinct phases, the first of which is to extract the morphine. The second step utilizes the extracted morphine as the raw material in a substitution reaction known as acetylation to create diacetylmorphine, a.k.a. heroin.

Since morphine is the starting material for heroin as well as an end product by itself, this chapter divides naturally into two section: morphine first and then heroin.

HEROIN MOLECULE

PART ONE: MORPHINE

THERE ARE TWO STEPS, TWO PROCEDURES FOR GETTING MORPHINE FROM opium: Extraction and Isolation (or Separation).

EXTRACTION: If you have ever made coffee, you are already familiar with extraction. To make a pot of coffee you use a solvent (water) to remove the caffeine, flavor and colored chemical compounds from the coffee bean. You use hot water because it dissolves more of the coffee chemicals than cold water, and to make the extraction more efficient and quicker, the beans are first ground up into small particles, exposing more surface area to the solvent. In a chemistry lab your cup of coffee might be called an aqueous solution of coffee alkaloids, congeners, oils, and flavor compounds.

ISOLATION: Isolation is what you'd do with the coffee if what you want is the caffeine by itself and nothing else from among all the other chemicals extracted into your pot of coffee. The usual approach to this problem is to take advantage of the particular characteristics of each constituent, then altering conditions so the one you want will separate from the others. Typical changes are made to the temperature, pH, or the addition of other chemicals... and figuring out what will work can be tedious.

Fortunately, morphine was the first alkaloid ever isolated and, in the more than two centuries since then, a lot of excellent methods have been devised to extract morphine from opium—among them are the ones covered here, which are all easily performed by non-scientist people, likely to produce good yields, and don't require any dangerous or exotic chemicals.

Brief Overview: "Lime water" extractions follow the same general route: First, the opium is dissolved in water and filtered to strain out twigs, dirt, or any other junk that may have gotten in it during the harvest. To this solution comes the addition of lime (calcium oxide) or "slaked lime" (calcium hydroxide) or a mixture of the two, which raises the pH to around 12, converting most of the opium alkaloids to a water-insoluble form so they drop out of solution to materialize as solid particles within the liquid.

While this happens to almost all the alkaloids, it doesn't work with morphine. Morphine is different than its sibling opium alkaloids—it doesn't precipitate for the most part and remains dissolved in the lime solution. So, after filtering to remove the unwanted alkaloids, the remaining liquid still contains the morphine (and a very small amount of codeine). To get the morphine out, the chemist adds ammonium chloride, which lowers the pH to between 8 and 9 and also changes morphine's solubility, causing it to precipitate out of solution, too.

After that, the morphine can be collected by another filtration, dried, and further purified—or turned into heroin.

CLASSICAL PROCESSES FOR OPIUM EXTRACTION

MERCK, ROBERTSON-GREGORY, THIBOUMERY AND MOHR

THREE "CLASSICAL PROCESSES" FOR EXTRACTING MORPHINE WERE DEveloped by nineteenth-century chemists for European companies to produce morphine using methods that were efficient, used cheap and available chemicals, and yielded a product of reliable and repeatable quality. These methods accomplished those goals for 150 years and more. Even today, clandestine heroin manufacturers from Thailand to Pakistan use procedures based on the Thiboumery and Mohr "lime water" process!

The following overview is taken from a 1950 survey of the classics by André Barbier. They are intended to provide a picture of successful approaches to extracting morphine but they aren't much good as step-by-step instructions. Typical of this sort of academic/scholarly chemistry articles, they lack sufficient detail and are written in a language that can be frustratingly vague and confusing.

For example, terms like "dilute acetic acid" cry out for clarification (how dilute is "dilute"?) and phrases like "until exhausted" or the ever-popular instruction to "treat" something can require an expert to interpret correctly. Comments within the text are intended to clarify such things when possible—they're not meant as corrections.

MERCK PROCESS: The opium is exhausted (washed) with cold water and the resultant liquor concentrated to a syrupy consistency. It is then precipitated hot with powdered sodium carbonate and heated as long as ammonia is given off; the solution should remain alkaline to phenolphthalein (above pH 9). After standing for 24 hours, the resultant precipitate is filtered and washed with cold water; when the wash water is colorless, the precipitate is dissolved in alcohol at 85 degrees. The alcoholic solution is evaporated, to dryness and the residue is exhausted by means of dilute acetic acid (vinegar), which is added in small quantities as neutralization proceeds. The acetic acid solution is treated with decolorizing charcoal, then filtered and precipitated with ammonia, care being taken to avoid an excess. The precipitate is filtered, washed, and purified by crystallization from alcohol; concentration of the alcoholic mother-liquor yields a further quantity of morphine.

ROBERTSON-GREGORY PROCESS: The opium is completely exhausted (extracted) by five to ten times its weight of cold water; the solution obtained is evaporated to the consistency of a soft extract, and then the process is repeated with cold distilled water. This aqueous re-extraction causes impurities to precipitate, they are filtered off—this filtering step is difficult since the filter paper becomes clogged, and the solution obtained is evaporated until its density is 10 degrees Baume (this is an old term describing specific gravity, which here would be 1.075). One hundred and twenty grammes (grams) of calcium chloride for each kilogram of opium are added to the boiling liquor which is then diluted with a quantity of cold water equal to its own volume. A precipitate of meconate and sulphate of calcium is thus formed and is filtered off. After filtering, the liquid is again concentrated, and this produces a new deposit which consists almost exclusively of calcium meconate. This deposit is filtered off and the solution is left standing. After a few days it becomes a crystalline mass composed of morphine hydrochloride and codeine hydrochloride: this is known as "Gregory's salt." The crystals obtained are drained and then placed in a cloth and squeezed out in a press. They are purified by successive crystallizations, the solutions being decolorized each time with animal charcoal. When the crystals are sufficiently pure, they are dissolved in water and the morphine is precipitated with ammonia; the codeine remains in solution.

According to Barbier, one drawback of this process is the 20 to 25 percent of the morphine is left with the secondary alkaloids in the brown and viscous mother-liquids after filtration of "Gregory's salt." Numerous modifications were developed to deal with such problems, among them the use of organic solvents, crystallization and repeated pressing to painstakingly retrieve the rest of the morphine and then each of the other alkaloids.

THIBOUMERY AND MOHR PROCESS: The opium is cut into thin slices and treated (dissolved) with three times its weight of hot water until a homogeneous paste is obtained. The (still hot) liquid is filtered, the residue pressed (squeezed, really, to get all the water out) and again treated with three times its weight of water. The solutions obtained are evaporated to half their volume and poured into boiling milk of lime: one part of lime (calcium oxide) in ten parts of water should be used for four parts of opium.

The precipitate is filtered off and re-treated with three parts of water to one part of opium; it is then filtered off again. The lime solutions are united (combined) and concentrated to a quantity twice the weight of the opium used. The solution is filtered, heated to boiling, and the morphine is precipitated by the addition of ammonium chloride (at a pH of between 8–9).

After cooling, it is filtered: the precipitate is washed, then purified by solution in hydrochloric acid and crystallization of the morphine hydrochloride. (Note: the lime used in this process is calcium oxide; caution should be observed when adding quicklime to water since it is an exothermic reaction.)

This process is an attractive one: there are no technical difficulties and the morphine is well separated from the secondary alkaloids: the morphine solutions are relatively clean. Barbier made certain changes in this process; for instance, instead of precipitating the lime solution with ammonium chloride, he acidified it slightly with hydrochloric acid and salted out the morphine hydrochloride with common salt. In this way he obtained almost all the morphine from the lime solution in the form of very pure hydrochloride. The morphine remaining in the salted-out liquid was precipitated and returned for purification.

MAKING HEROIN OUT OF MOM'S CODEINE PILLS

By Rhodium 980729

INTRODUCTION

This text deals with four known methods of converting codeine to morphine by demethylation (codeine is morphine 3-methyl ether). Cleavage of aromatic ethers are commonly effected by reflux with concentrated HBr or HI. This relatively simple method can unfortunately not be used on codeine, as the oxygen bridge at the 9,10-position on the morphinan carbon skeleton would also rupture, causing the rearrangement of the molecule to the very potent emetic apomorphine, completely devoid of opiate-like effects. The author takes no responsibility whatsoever of whatever the reader might do with the information contained in this document. Keep in mind that the procedures described herein are probably illegal to carry out in all civilized parts of the world. Suggestions of alternative demethylation methods or anecdotal reports of the use of the syntheses below are welcomed.

USING PYRIDINE HCL[1,2]

A mixture of 1.00 g. of codeine and 3 g. of pyridine hydrochloride was placed in a bath at 220°C and heated for six minutes in a nitrogen atmosphere, after which the reaction mixture was immediately cooled and dissolved in 20 ml of water, basified with 10 ml of 4 N sodium hydroxide, and the non-phenolic material was removed by extraction with four 15-ml portions of chloroform. The combined chloroform extracts were washed with 10 ml of 0.5 N sodium hydroxide and 10 ml of water, and the aqueous phase, after adding the washings, was adjusted to pH 9 and cooled thoroughly to precipitate phenolic material. After filtering and drying, this phenolic material was digested with 75 ml of methanol, the mixture was filtered hot and the filtrate was chromatographed on an alumina (Merck) column (120x11 mm) using 700 ml of methanol as eluent. The residue after evaporation of the methanol was dissolved in 10 ml of 0.2 N sodium hydroxide, filtered, and the filtrate was adjusted to pH 9, precipitating the crude morphine. After drying, this crude morphine was sublimed (180–190°C (0.1 mm)), and the sublimate was crystallized from absolute ethanol. There was thus obtained a total of 210 mg. (22%) of morphine, mp 254–255°C.

THE "HOMEBAKE" METHOD[3]

This is excerpted from a report dealing with clandestine manufacture of morphine and heroin from OTC codeine remedies, in so-called "homebake" laboratories in New Zealand. The method used is the same as the one introduced by Rapoport in 1951[1], using pyridine hydrochloride. The authors report some perps' claims of 50% conversion from the codeine, but say they obtained 30% typically, and further state that this is about what one would expect from Rapoport's paper. Purity of up to 92% with a more typical purity in the 80% range was reported by the forensic chemists evaluating the method.

The following is the procedure reportedly used in the clandestine labs, with some elaboration:

• Crush sufficient pills to yield 2 g of codeine and mix with distilled water. Filter with a vacuum funnel to remove insolubles and add to a separatory funnel. Add NaOH solution to make the solution pH 12. Extract twice with chloroform (2x25 ml). This will be the bottom layer. Discard the water layer, which contains the aspirin or acetaminophen, and evaporate the chloroform layer to dryness under gentle heat. The result is codeine base, a white crystalline powder.

• Combine 20 ml pyridine and 25 ml conc. HCl in a beaker and heat strongly to 190°C to drive off any water. Cover and cool rapidly to obtain a white waxy material. This should be stored in a sealed container in the freezer if not to be used immediately.

• The reaction is carried out in a glass boiling tube (here one could use a large-ignition type test tube) which is sealed on one end. This should be oven-dried before use. Then 3.5 g of the pyridine salt is added to the tube and this is then heated until it melts and for a few minutes more to drive off any moisture. Add 1.5 g of the base and seal the tube with a rubber stopper covered with a filter paper. Heat until the mixture begins to fume and continue until the mixture develops a reddish-orange color and becomes noticeably more viscous, typically 6–12 minutes.

• Pour this into a 500 ml sep funnel and make the volume up to 100 mL with distilled water. Add 10% NaOH until strongly basic. The contents will become milky brown and then clear brown as the solution is made basic. When this point is reached, extract with 20 ml chloroform. This will contain any unreacted codeine (up to 70%) and may be saved for recovery if desired. The morphine is in the water layer.

• Put the water layer in a beaker and carefully adjust the pH with HCl to pH 9 using a narrow range pHydronium paper. This is critical. Rapidly filter using two layers of paper (here one could use a paper designed for very fine crystals) and a vacuum flask/funnel as in step 1. A very fine brown powder will collect on the paper. This is unwanted byproducts and should be discarded.

• Pour the filtrate into a clean beaker and, while carefully adjusting the pH to 8.5, vigorously rubbing the inside of the beaker with a "seeding stick" (here the authors mention that a split wooden peg is *sometimes used in the home labs in NZ; a glass stirring rod would be preferable). Crystals should begin to form. These are allowed to settle for at least 5 minutes and then are recovered by vacuum filtering to recover the morphine as a beige to dark brown product.*

REPORT FROM SOMEONE USING THE ABOVE METHOD:

USING BORON TRIBROMIDE[4]

A solution of 2.99g (10 mmol) of anhydrous codeine in 25 ml of CHCl3 was added during 2 min to a well-stirred solution of 15g (59.9 mmol) of BBr3 in 175 ml of CHCl3 maintained in the range 23–26°C. A 10-ml portion of CHCl3, which was used to rinse the addition funnel, was added to the reaction mixture and stirring was continued for 15 min at 23–26°C. The reaction mixture was then poured into a well-stirred mixture of 80g ice and 20 ml of concentrated (28–30%) ammonia. The two-phase system was kept at -5°C to 0°C for 0.5h (continous stirring) and filtered. The resulting crystalline material was washed thoroughly with small portions of cold CHCl3 and H2O and dried to give 2.67g (88.1%) of slightly off-white morphine hydrate, mp 252.5–254°C.

REPORT FROM A CHEMIST TRYING OUT THE ABOVE METHOD:

I extracted the codeine using the NaOH/chloroform method. I then went through the synthesis—the BBr3 is really nasty—fuming toxic shit! I had a high-power exhaust fan in front of my work area and it took care of the fumes (all the insects outside the window died!). I dissolved the BBr3 in chloroform and then added the codeine/chloroform mixture—lots of HBr gas evolved—stoppered the flask and led the fumes into water, which dissolved the HBr gas. The codeine made this funky pink precipitate. Continued to follow the steps, added mix to ammonia/ice (I had this in a alcohol/ice bath at -5°C). Once again fumes evolved (not as much). Stirred 30 min. Filtered out a pale white-yellow gelatinous material, washed with cold chloroform and water and dried. It seemed to have a bromine odor and was very acidic (I probably used a bit too much BBr3) so I washed with cold water again (morphine hydrate isn't water soluble) and the pH normalized. I then dissolved it in dilute HCl, and neutralized to pH 6 with NaOH.

I'm going to be more precise with amounts etc. next time, and hopefully this will improve the yield (now it was only 50%!).

Using Sodium Propylmercaptide[5]

A solution of 3.00 grams (10 mmol) of codeine in 60 ml of dry dimethylformamide was degassed under nitrogen by repeatedly stirring under vacuum, followed by inletting nitrogen. Following the addition of 3.00 grams (26.7 mmol) of potassium tert-butoxide, the degassing process was repeated, and 3.0 ml (32.7 mmol) of n-propanethiol was injected by syringe. The mixture was stirred at 125°C under nitrogen for 45 min (similar results at 110°C for 3h), cooled, and quenched with 3.0 ml of acetic acid. The solvent was removed under high vacuum, and the residue dissolved in 30 ml of 1N hydrochloric acid. The acid solution was washed with several portions of ether, treated with 5ml of 20% sodium bisulfite, and alkalized to pH 9 with ammonium hydroxide. The precipitated solid was collected, washed with water, and dried in vacuo (100°C) to leave 2.30g (80%) of morphine as tan crystals.

Using L-Selectride (Lithium tri-sec-butyl Hydride)[6,7]

482 mg (1.6 mmol) of codeine was dissolved in 4 ml of an 1 M solution of L-selectride in THF (4.0 mmol) and was refluxed for 3.5h. The reaction was quenched with water (5ml), followed by 2ml of 15% NaOH solution and removal of the THF. The resulting mixture was washed twice with CH_2Cl_2, cooled to 0–5°C and

acidified to pH 1 with 10% HCl. After basification with ammonium hydroxide to pH 9, the mixture was extracted into CHCl$_3$, the organic phase was washed with brine and dried over Na$_2$SO$_4$. Removal of the solvent, followed by recrystallization from water gave 355mg (73%) of morphine hydrate. Unreacted codeine was recovered from the non-phenolic extracts, and after purification by recrystallization from water, it amounted to 71mg (14%).

REFERENCES

• H. Rapoport, **The Preparation of Morphine-N-Methyl-C**[14], J. Am. Chem. Soc., 73, 5900 (1951)

• H. Rapoport, **Delta-7-Desoxymorphine**, J. Am. Chem. Soc., 73, 5485 (1951)

• K. Bedford, **Illicit Preparation of Morphine from Codeine in NZ**, Forensic Sci. Int. 34(3), 197–204 (1987)

• K.C. Rice, **A Rapid, High-Yield Conversion of Codeine to Morphine**, J. Med. Chem., 20(1), 164 (1977)

• J.A. Lawson, **An Improved Method for O-Demethylation of Codeine**, J. Med. Chem., 20(1), 165 (1977)

• A. Coop, **L-selectride for the O-Demethylation of Opium Alkaloids**, J. Org. Chem., 63, 4392–96 (1998)

• G. Majetisch, **Hydride-Promoted Demethylation of Methyl Ethers**, Tet. Lett. 35(47), 8727–8730 (1994)

PART II: HEROIN

In the last part of the nineteenth century, the German chemical industry had begun to produce synthetic dyes which took over the world's dye market so quickly that they neared the limits of growth in that area. When the German corporation Bayer's chemists discovered a way to turn coal tar waste into headache medicine, the firm went into the pharmaceutical business and in 1899 introduced the world to a new medication, including its trademarked Heroin.

Heroin had already been discovered a couple of times before Bayer, the first time in 1874 by C.R.A. Wright at St. Elizabeth's Hospital in London. After carrying out an acetylation reaction on morphine, Wright took some of what he'd made and fed it to a dog. He noted its reactions (rectal temperature dropped a few degrees, he tells us) and, apparently unimpressed, didn't go any further with the experiment.

It wasn't till 1898 that heroin was officially discovered by Theodore Dreser of the Bayer Co., who had already chalked up one success acetylating salicylic acid to synthesize a compound Bayer would call Aspirin. Bayer, however, did a lot more testing on heroin. Among the first to try out the drug were some healthy young lads recruited to help establish what an effective dose of the stuff might be. Then, scores of Bayer employees were given the drug and its effects were obvious: it was a lot like morphine, but a good two or even three times stronger.

Heroin is made from morphine by substituting an acetyl group (COOH) on the alcohol (OH) groups at the molecule's 3 and 6 positions, thus transforming morphine into diacetylmorphine, or heroin. That is the entire difference between morphine and heroin. Yet the effect is to make the drug much more bioavailable and consequently two or three times stronger. Some of this analgesia is due to its increased ability to enter the brain, get metabolized to morphine and start to work. But some of it appears to also be a result of its metabolite 6-MAM, which has been shown to be four times as strong as plain morphine.

The same procedure used to produce aspirin from a willow bark extract is also used to turn morphine into heroin. In fact, the acetylation procedures for making aspirin and heroin are so similar, any aspirin synthesis can be used as a guide to making heroin—just substitute morphine for salicylic acid. The relative amounts of acetic anhydride are the same, as are the reaction times and other conditions.

THE GOLDEN TRIANGLE METHOD: The procedure comes to us courtesy of the DEA, which published a booklet entitled "Heroin Manufacture in Southeast Asia" in 1993, whose anonymous author(s) outlined their observations of anonymous clandestine heroin manufacturers in an undisclosed location within the Golden Triangle. The publication appears to have been a byproduct of research done by multiple agencies of the U.S. government engaged in developing a way to locate and accurately assess opium poppy crops from satellites.

Before it describes how morphine is extracted, it explains how opium is first processed ("cooked"). This is done to wash away dirt and plant material in preparation for extraction but it also creates a product known as "smoking opium" of the sort favored by Chinese people ever since Britain first brought the stuff from India.

The booklet may still be available online but it's hard to know for certain that any online version you find is correct, or complete or free from deliberate misinformation. The following is taken from an original copy of the publication.

"COOKING OPIUM": *Before opium is smoked, it is usually cooked. Uncooked opium contains moisture, as well as soil, leaves, twigs, and other impurities that diminish the quality of the final product. The raw opium collected from the opium poppy pods is placed in an open cooking pot of boiling water where the sticky globs of opium alkaloids* quickly dissolve. Soil, twigs, plant scrapings, etc., remain undissolved. The solution is then strained through cheesecloth to remove these impurities. The clear brown liquid that remains is opium in solution, sometimes called "liquid opium." This liquid is then re-heated over a low flame until the water is driven off into the air as steam leaving a thick dark brown paste. This paste is called "prepared," "cooked," or "smoking" opium. It is dried in the sun until it has a putty-like consistency. The net weight of the cooked opium is generally only 80 percent that of the original raw opium. Thus, cooked opium is more pure than its original, raw form, and has a higher monetary value.

Cooked opium is suitable for smoking or eating by opium users. Traditionally there is only one group of opium poppy farmers, the Hmong, who prefer not to cook their opium before smoking. Most other ethnic groups, including Chinese opium addicts, prefer smoking cooked opium. If the opium is to be sold to traders for use in morphine or heroin laboratories, it is not necessary to cook it first. The laboratory operators generally use 55-gallon oil drums or huge cooking vats to dissolve the raw opium before beginning the morphine extraction process.

"EXTRACTION OF MORPHINE": Raw or cooked opium contains more than 35 different alkaloids, including morphine, which accounts for approximately 10 percent of the total raw opium weight. Heroin manufacturers must first extract the morphine from the opium before converting the morphine to heroin. The extraction is a simple process, requiring only a few chemicals and a supply of water. Since the morphine base is about one-tenth the weight and volume of raw opium, it is desirable to reduce the opium to morphine before transporting the product any great distance. Morphine is sometimes extracted from opium in small clandestine "laboratories," which may be set up near the opium poppy fields. The process of extracting morphine from opium involves dissolving opium in hot water, adding lime to precipitate the non-morphine alkaloids and then adding ammonium chloride to precipitate the morphine from the solution. An empty oil drum and some cooking pots are all that is needed. The following is a step-by-step description of morphine extraction in a typical Southeast Asian laboratory: An empty 55-gallon oil drum is placed on bricks about a foot above the ground and a fire is built under the drum. Thirty gallons of water are added to the drum and brought to a boil. Ten to 15 kilograms of raw opium are added to the boiling water. With stirring, the raw opium eventually dissolves in the boiling water, while soil, leaves, twigs, and other non-soluble materials float in the solution. Most of these materials are scooped out of the clear brown "liquid opium" solution. Slaked lime (calcium hydroxide), or more often a readily available chemical fertilizer with a high content of lime, is added to the solution. The lime converts the water insoluble morphine into the water-soluble calcium morphenate. The other opium alkaloids do not react with the lime to form soluble calcium salts. Codeine is slightly water soluble and gets carried over with the calcium morphenate in the liquid. For the most part, the other alkaloids become part of the residual sediment "sludge" that comes to rest on the bottom of the oil drum. As the solution cools, and after the insolubles precipitate out, the morphine solution is scooped from the drum and poured through a filter of some kind. Burlap rice sacks are often used as filters. They are later squeezed in a press to remove most of the solution from the wet sacks. The solution is then poured into large cooking pots and re-heated, but not boiled. Ammonium chloride is added to the heated calcium morphenate solution to adjust the alkalinity to a pH of 8 to 9, and the solution is then allowed to cool. Within one or two hours, the morphine base and the unextracted codeine base precipitate out of the solution and settle to the bottom of the cooking pot. The solution is then poured off through cloth filters. Any solid morphine base chunks in the solution will remain on the cloth. The morphine base is removed from both the cooking pot and from the filter cloths, wrapped and squeezed in cloth, and then dried in the sun. When dry, the crude morphine base is a coffee-colored powder. This 'crude' morphine base, commonly known by the Chinese term throughout Southeast Asia, may be further purified by dissolving it in hydrochloric acid, adding activated charcoal, re-heating and re-filtering. The solution is filtered several more times, and the morphine (morphine hydrochloride) is then dried in the sun. Morphine hydrochloride (still tainted with codeine hydrochloride) is usually formed into small brick-sized blocks in a press and wrapped in paper or cloth. The most common block size is 2 inches by 4 inches by 5 inches weighing about 1.3 kilograms (3 lbs). The bricks are then dried for transport to heroin processing laboratories. Approximately 13 kilograms of opium, from one hectare of opium poppies, are needed to produce each morphine block of this size. The morphine blocks are bundled and packed for transport to heroin laboratories by human couriers or by pack animals. Pack mules are able to carry 100-kilogram payloads over 200 miles of rugged mountain trails in less than three weeks.

❖

HEROIN MANUFACTURING IN AFGHANISTAN

The following information is taken from an article called "Documentation of a Heroin Manufacturing Process in Afghanistan" by U. Zerell, B. Ahrens and P. Gerz of the Federal Criminal Police Office, Wiesbaden, Germany.

Their explanation of the way heroin is manufactured from opium is so thorough and clear that it's not possible to improve upon it. The article was published by the United Nations in 2005 and as such, is not protected by copyright. For a copy of the entire article, along with its helpful photographs of various steps in the process see www.unodc.org/pdf/.../bulletin_on_narcotics_2007_Zerell.pdf .

This particular procedure makes little use of any solvents besides water and its use of other chemicals is kept to a minimum, yet this isn't done at the expense of the end products.

Abstract

The present article includes a description of all stages of the heroin manufacturing process, followed by a flow chart summarizing those steps and listing the intermediate products and the chemicals needed. Explanations given and the names of substances used were confirmed by means of forensic analysis and expert knowledge. Finally, the process is discussed with reference to published accounts of manufacturing methods.

EXTRACTING THE MORPHINE FROM RAW OPIUM:

The raw opium was unwrapped, crushed and divided into two por-
tions. The wrapping material was not entirely removed. The crushed
opium was poured into two barrels and hot water was added.

The composition was stirred until it became a homogeneous
suspension. The pH value was 8. The remaining plastic wrapping
floated to the surface of the liquid and was scooped out. Then calcium
oxide (anhydrous lime) was added, together with more hot water.
The suspension was stirred well from time to time, for a period that
lasted about an hour. During that period, sometimes hot water and
sometimes a solution of calcium oxide (anhydrous lime) and hot water
were used to rinse off any opium still stuck to the wrapping material.
The rinsing solution was poured into the barrels containing the main
substance. The barrels were then filled with hot water and left to stand
overnight. By the next morning, a brownish foam residue and an oily
film had appeared on the surface of the morphine solution. The pH
value was measured at between 10 and 12. In the course of the extrac-
tion process, other water-soluble substances were co-extracted with the
morphine. Separating the morphine solution from the water-insoluble

opium components A hose was used to siphon the clear, dark brown morphine solution into two tubs.

After that, the solution was divided into four empty barrels. The sediment was stirred up, ladled out of the barrels with buckets and filtered through sacks that had been soaked in water. The entire filtrate was then poured back into the four barrels containing the morphine solution.

TREATMENT OF THE WATER-INSOLUBLE OPIUM CONSTITUENTS

The sacks containing the opium residue were placed in a pressing device, and the liquid was squeezed out of them. The liquid pressed from the sacks was added to the barrels containing the morphine solution. Then the press cake was removed from the sacks, divided in two parts, put in two barrels and treated with hot water to dissolve out more morphine. After being filtered and pressed, the additional liquid extracted from the sacks was also added to the main morphine solution.

Precipitation, Isolation and Drying of the Morphine

Then ammonium chloride was added to each barrel while stirring continuously. The morphine base precipitated. The barrels were covered and left to stand overnight.

The next morning, the morphine base was filtered using two filtering baskets lined with cloth that had been soaked in warm water. The solution had a pH value of 9. The main morphine base substance, which was in the sediment, was stirred using some of the remaining liquid, thus producing a suspension. The suspension was then filtered out, and the filtrate was discarded. The moist morphine base remained in the cloth-lined filtering baskets. The morphine base was wrapped in the filtering cloths and stamped out.

Finally, the morphine base was spread out on a cloth to dry. Then, the air-dried morphine base was weighed.

CONVERSION OF MORPHINE TO HEROIN

The amount of acetic anhydride needed for heroin synthesis was weighed out. (For the quantities of the chemicals used, see the section entitled "Laboratory equipment and chemicals" below.)

Then the acetic anhydride was added to the morphine base, which had been placed in an aluminum pot. A small excess of the chemical was added. The pot was stirred until the morphine base had dissolved. The pot was covered, and the reaction solution was allowed to stand for 45 minutes. Then the pot was placed on a fire, and the reaction solution was heated for another 30 minutes.

After that, the reaction mixture was poured into a bowl that had been filled with hot water. Then the solution was filtered through a cloth, and the filtered solution was poured into an empty barrel.

PRECIPITATION AND ISOLATION OF THE BROWN HEROIN BASE

Portions of sodium carbonate solution were poured into the barrel until gas was no longer released and the heroin base precipitated out. The precipitated heroin base was immediately filtered out. The pH value of the solution was 10. The heroin base was then stirred up in hot water and filtered again. The washing process was repeated once more. Then the brown heroin base was poured into a bowl.

PURIFICATION OF THE BROWN HEROIN BASE

The brown heroin base was dissolved in diluted hydrochloric acid. The solution had a pH value of 7-8. Because not all of the heroin base had dissolved, the solution was filtered through a cloth. Activated carbon was then stirred into the solution, and the liquid was allowed to stand for 30 minutes. Then the activated carbon was filtered out using a cloth. Because the solution was not yet clear, it was filtered a second time, using a paper filter.

Precipitation and isolation of the white heroin base

Then, the heroin base was precipitated using a diluted ammonia solution. The pH value was 12. The white heroin base was filtered through a cloth. Conversion of the heroin base to heroin hydrochloride The white heroin base was dissolved in a mixture containing hydrochloric acid and a small amount of acetone. The heroin solution was then filtered through a paper filter into a metal bowl and evaporated on a water bath. The white heroin hydrochloride precipitated.

Discussion

Currently, there are few publicly available descriptions of the processes used to make illicit heroin. The production processes, for which only very general descriptions are provided, use the Thiboumery and Mohr method, also known as the lime method ([1], p. 6) for the first step of extracting morphine from opium.

For example, Cooper [2] reported on the illicit production of heroin based on the extraction of morphine base using hot water and adding calcium oxide, followed by precipitation with ammonium chloride. The conversion to heroin base occurs by adding a large excess of acetic anhydride to the dried morphine base and heating it for 30 minutes. A further conversion to heroin hydrochloride is not described.

Recent publications of the United Nations Office on Drugs and Crime provide flow charts [3] and schematic presentations [4] of the illicit manufacturing of heroin preparations and refer to the main features of the Thiboumery and Mohr method as well as the use of organic solvents in an optional purification step for morphine isolation and the conversion of morphine into heroin hydrochloride. A report of the International Narcotics Control Board (INCB) presents a similar, but greatly simplified, flow chart for illicit manufacture of heroin hydrochloride [5].

The extraction of morphine base during the process observed by the authors was based, for the most part, on the Thiboumery and Mohr method. Unlike in the production process mentioned above, the morphine base was not purified with charcoal. That first purification step was carried out at the stage of the heroin base, that is, after the morphine had been converted to heroin. In this process, only a very small quantity of organic solvent was used, when the purified heroin base was transformed into heroin hydrochloride.

The persons processing the heroin identified the chemicals by their external characteristics such as odour and appearance. Sparing use was made of all chemicals required for the production process, with the exception of water. Only a minute quantity of an organic solvent was used. Hot water was used as a solvent throughout the production process. Only a small quantity of the substance referred to as the "key chemical", acetic anhydride, was used. That amount was so small that it was at the bottom of the range of quantities of acetic anhydride reported to have been used in the process elsewhere. According to the

*persons processing the heroin, in this case, the fact that such a small
quantity was used was not the consequence of a lack of availability of
the chemical; they considered the amount sufficient for the traditional
method that they used to make heroin.*

ANALYSIS OF THE
DOCUMENTED PROCESS

YIELD

*Some 7.8 kg of morphine base were obtained from 70 kg of raw
opium, which is a yield of 11 percent in terms of the weight of the
raw opium. The yield of the final product, white heroin hydrochloride
of 74 per cent purity, was 3.9 kg, that is, 6 percent of the weight of
the raw opium (see figure II). It was not possible to weigh the brown
and the white heroin bases during the production process, because
they were not dried but directly processed while wet. In the literature,
there are few instances in which the yield obtained at each step of the
illicit heroin manufacture process is specified. According to UNODC
[1], 10 kg of opium yields about 1 kg of morphine base—a yield of
10 per cent—which is considered to produce, in turn, about 1 kg of
heroin base. The quantity of the morphine base produced using the
method documented in this article is almost identical to that published
quantity. However, the more recent UNODC data indicate a higher
morphine content in raw opium from Afghanistan. Because of this
and/or increased laboratory efficiency, a higher yield reportedly can be
achieved, with a conversion ratio of between 7:1 and 6:1 [6]. For the
above reasons, in the manufacture process documented, no measure-
ment of the yield of heroin base could be made to compare with the
data provided by UNODC.*

The materials were weighed on location using a beam balance and weights that CNPA had borrowed from a local trader. Because the lightest weight was 500 grams, it was not possible to establish the exact weight of the materials. Thus, weights had to be estimated using expert knowledge. However, the quantity of acetic anhydride used could be precisely determined, because the weight of the acetic anhydride was established on the basis of the weight of the morphine base used. Due to its sticky consistency, the raw opium was weighed together with its wrapping material.

ANALYSIS OF ACTIVE INGREDIENTS

The samples of the raw opium, the morphine base, the press cake, the brown heroin base, the white heroin base and the white heroin hydrochloride were transferred to polyethylene containers at the production site and stored at room temperature until they were analyzed in Germany, at the Forensic Science Institute of BKA. Before the samples were analyzed, they were dried over phosphorus pentoxide until their weight remained constant, except for the raw opium samples and the morphine base, which were analyzed immediately. The raw opium, the morphine base and the press cake were analyzed to determine their active ingredients (see table 3).

The raw opium used was made up of four visually distinguishable quantities. The persons preparing the heroin examined the raw opium and said that they were not satisfied with it because it was of poor quality. Dry weights were used, except for the alkaloid content of the raw opium, for which the undried weight was used. The additional drying of the raw opium at 110 °C to a constant weight led to no significant change in the alkaloid content. The average opium alkaloid content in dried, raw opium [1] is: morphine, 11.4 per cent (range: 3.1-19.2 per cent); codeine, 3.5 per cent (range: 0.7-6.6 per cent); papaverine, 3.2 per cent (range: <0.1-9.0 per cent); and narcotine, 8.1 per cent *(range:1.4-15.8 per cent). A more recent report from UNODC states that the morphine content of raw opium from Afghanistan ranges from 8.4 to 23.5 per cent [6]. The average morphine content of the raw opium used in the process documented is somewhat lower than those published values; that confirms the assessment made by the persons demonstrating this method of processing heroin.*

The very lower residual morphine content of the press cake (0.2 per cent) indicates that almost all the alkaloid content was extracted from the raw opium used.

The brown heroin base, the white heroin base and the white heroin hydrochloride were analyzed to determine their alkaloid content (see table 4).

A relatively high monoacetylmorphine content (5.4-7.8 per cent) was found in the samples of the brown heroin base, the white heroin base and the white heroin hydrochloride. That could be a result of hydrolysis: because of the cool, rainy weather at the time of synthesis, it was not possible to completely dry the samples. According to the persons who demonstrated this method of heroin processing, intermediate products are usually directly processed or, as in the case of the morphine base, laid out and air-dried.

Comparison with heroin analysis program data The results of the chemical analysis of the composition of main and trace substances contained in the samples taken from the documented manufacture process are compared with data from the heroin analysis program and discussed below.

MORPHINE BASE

The morphine base of the process observed in Kabul had a purity of 53.1 per cent. Morphine base has been seized in only a few cases in Germany. A total of 10 sets of data on samples of this type were stored in the database of the heroin analysis program Those samples had an

average purity of 59.0 per cent, with a range of 38.4-83.6 per cent.
The sample from Kabul has a similar average purity. The same is true
for the content of the opium alkaloids codeine and papaverine. The
10 database samples had an average codeine content of 5.0 per cent
(range: 2.3-6.8 per cent) and an average papaverine content of 2.2
per cent (range: 0.6-3.8 per cent). The narcotine content of the 10
database samples varied widely, from 0.3 to 60.3 per cent. However,
the average narcotine content, 21.4 per cent, was almost identical to
that of the sample from Kabul.

BROWN HEROIN BASE

The database of the heroin analysis program contained 925 sets of data
for undiluted and unadulterated brown heroin base from South-West
Asia. There is no analytical information or intelligence on heroin of
this type coming from South-East Asia.

   The brown heroin base from Kabul has a diacetylmorphine content
of 68.1 per cent (see table 4), which is higher than the average value of
53.7 per cent (range: 12.2-89.0 per cent) of the 925 database sets. In
contrast, the narcotine content of the Kabul sample is relatively low:
6.0 per cent. The narcotine content of the database samples ranges
from not detectable to 66.8 per cent. This shows that the narcotine
must have been lost directly after acetylation (the reaction with acetic
anhydride), either during the hydrolysis of the excess acetic anhydride
(when adding the reaction solution to water) or during the precipitation
of the heroin base. The brown heroin base from Kabul corresponds to
the pattern of South-West Asian heroin, which predominates in the
heroin preparations seized in Germany. A singular characteristic of
the Kabul sample is its low narcotine content: 6.0 per cent (see table
4). The sets of data on samples attributed to South-West Asia have
an average narcotine content of 21.8 per cent. Of the 925 sets of
data from the database, only seven had similar ratios of total morphine

(sum of the percentages of diacetylmorphine, monoacetylmorphine and morphine) to acetylcodeine, total morphine to papaverine, total morphine to narcotine and papaverine to narcotine, which made those samples suitable for comparison on the basis of the composition of the main ingredients. Five of the seven data sets came from data sheets; so, in those cases there were no actual samples available for additional examination (the comparison of the trace profiles). The trace profiles of the two remaining samples with a similar composition of main components, however, differed greatly from the trace profile of the brown heroin base from Kabul. Thus, it was not possible to find a comparable heroin preparation in the collection of BKA. The brown heroin base from Kabul is a variation of the South-West Asian type of heroin that had not been detected in Germany before.

WHITE HEROIN BASE

The white heroin base has a clearly higher diacetylmorphine content than the brown heroin base: 78.5 per cent. In the process observed, the purification of the heroin preparation with the help of activated carbon was effective: an additional separation of papaverine and narcotine was achieved in the course of that processing stage.

The database of the heroin analysis programme does not contain data on white heroin base samples. It is not known whether such preparations have appeared yet in the drug scene in Germany. Probably, white heroin base is an intermediate product of white heroin hydrochloride manufacture that does not usually appear on the illicit market. The persons demonstrating how heroin was prepared confirmed that assumption when they said that they had never heard of anyone ordering that product.

The conversion of the white heroin base to the final product of white heroin hydrochloride resulted in a slight decrease in the diacetylmorphine content, from 78.5 to 74.0 per cent. That could easily be explained by the additional dissolving and filtering process.

The heroin analysis program collection contains 11 preparations of white heroin hydrochloride from 2002 and 2003 that have a similar diacetylmorphine content. None of those samples have a composition equivalent to the white hydrochloride from Kabul. The white heroin hydrochloride manufactured in the observed process is not identical to the type of heroin that is usually seized in Germany. As a rule, what is found in Germany is brown heroin base, which, in the manufacture process demonstrated, is no more than an intermediate product. The so-called "white heroin" seized occasionally in Germany since 2000 is white or off-white heroin hydrochloride with a pur calculated as base, believed to come from the South-West Asian region. Until now, it was unknown in which country that heroin preparation was produced. As the final product in Kabul shares key features of that "white heroin", it is clear that this kind of heroin can be produced in Afghanistan.

ADDITIONAL FINDINGS

Upon questioning, the two Afghans who demonstrated the heroin manufacturing process provided valuable forensic information on the set-up and organization of a clandestine heroin laboratory in Afghanistan. They explained that they themselves did not own a clandestine heroin laboratory but had been hired by a person operating a laboratory and that that person also provided the equipment and the chemicals. They gave no information about the usual size of such laboratories or their production capacity. They said that the person ordering the heroin manufacture would provide the person running the laboratory with the base material, raw opium, in plastic bags in the form of "opium bread" weighing approximately 0.5-1 kilogram, which would be bundled and put into larger plastic bags weighing one "khaltar" (approximately 7 kg). Several "khaltar" would then be put in a sack for transport. The conclusion to be drawn from that is that the raw opium that is converted to heroin can consist of multiple batches of varying quality coming from different areas of production. The person ordering the narcotic drug also decides which product is to be manufactured and monitors the manufacture process. The preparation of the morphine base and its subsequent conversion to heroin do not have to take place at the same laboratory. The manufacture itself takes place around the clock, without interruption, with a typical manufacture time of about 2-3 days. The process demonstrated by the two Afghans took about 50 hours. It became clear from talking with the two Afghans and observing them that their work was the result of acquired skills communicated orally. They carried out all steps with great care and skill. It can be assumed, however, that they did not have any scientific training. They did not reveal whether they were able to use other methods of processing heroin.

Conclusion

An authentic process of heroin production in Afghanistan was documented. White heroin hydrochloride was manufactured using simple and widely available equipment and a small quantity of chemicals. The quantities of chemicals actually used corresponded to the minimum required for processing heroin. The only organic solvent used was acetone, and only a very small quantity of it was used. The brown heroin base prepared as an intermediate product during the manufacture process shares some characteristics with the South-West Asian-type of heroin preparations usually seized in Germany.

Previously, it had not been possible to confirm the hypothesis that heroin with a high purity level ("white heroin") seized in countries in Western Europe, including Germany, could be from Afghanistan, as suggested by police investigations, because samples of heroin seized in Afghanistan had not been available for forensic analysis. The final product of the heroin manufacture process documented in this article was white heroin hydrochloride, which, forensic analysis has revealed, shares the key features of the "white heroin" occasionally seized in Germany since 2000. Thus, it has been proved that this type of heroin can be produced in Afghanistan. The question remains whether white heroin is manufactured in other countries as well.

The authors were unable to determine whether the documented manufacture process is typical of Afghanistan because it is the only authentic heroin manufacture process that BKA of Germany has so far documented. The way in which the two Afghans prepared the heroin suggested that it was a commonly used method. The question remains whether other methods of processing heroin exist and, if so, how many. Nevertheless, the information gained provides numerous clues about the amount of heroin that can be produced from opium and the quantities of chemicals required.

The documentation of the heroin manufacture process has provided useful insight into the operations of clandestine heroin laboratories. That information will be used for training forensic scientists and drug law enforcement officers. The information obtained in the course of the demonstration with regard to the chemicals used (their origin, type, amount, utilization, disguise and counterfeiting) supports operational drug enforcement measures. For example, as stated above in this article, smuggled chemicals are deceptively labeled or put in containers intended for other chemicals. It is hoped that making use of all this information in law enforcement operations will help reduce heroin manufacture in Afghanistan, although such a reduction clearly depends, first and foremost, on social conditions in Afghanistan itself. ❖

REFERENCES

1. *Recommended Methods for Testing Opium, Morphine and Heroin: Manual for Use by National Drug Testing Laboratories (ST/NAR/29/Rev.1).*

2. D. A. Cooper, "Clandestine production processes for cocaine and heroin in clandestinely produced drugs, analogues and precursors: problems and solutions", M. Klein and others, eds., *Proceedings of the International Conference on Assessment of Drug Control Issues of Controlled Substance Analogues, Rabat, 8-11 September 1987 (Washington, D.C., United States Department of Justice, Drug Enforcement Administration, 1989)*, pp. 95-116.

3. *Clandestine Manufacture of Substances under International Control: Manual for Use by National Law Enforcement and Narcotics Laboratory Personnel (ST/NAR/10/Rev.2)*, p. 167.

4. *The Opium Economy in Afghanistan: an International Problem (United Nations publication, Sales No. E.03.XI.6)*, p. 133.

5. *Precursors and Chemicals Frequently Used in the Illicit Manufacture of Narcotic Drugs and Psychotropic Substances: Report of the International Narcotics Control Board for 2004 on the Implementation of Article 12 of the United Nations Convention against Illicit Traffic in Narcotic Drugs and Psychotropic Substances of 1988 (United Nations publication, Sales No. E.05.XI.6)*, p. 77.

6. United Nations Office on Drugs and Crime, *Limited Opium Yield Assessment Surveys—Technical Report: Observations and Findings; Guidance for Future Activities* (2003).

Opium is the femme fatale, the pagodas, the lanterns!
I do not have the strength to undeceive you. Since science
does not know how to distinguish between the curative and
the destructive properties of opium, I must yield to it.

— Jean Cocteau, Opium —